The Pastor
Wears a Skirt

The Pastor Wears a Skirt

Stories of Gender and Ministry

Dorothy Nickel Friesen

With love + wisdom!

Dorothy NF

4/30/19

The man behind the book

Roland

RESOURCE *Publications* · Eugene, Oregon

THE PASTOR WEARS A SKIRT
Stories of Gender and Ministry

Resource Publications
An Imprint of Wipf and Stock Publishers
199 W. 8th Ave., Suite 3
Eugene, OR 97401

www.wipfandstock.com

PAPERBACK ISBN: 978-1-5326-4723-9
HARDCOVER ISBN: 978-1-5326-5040-6
EBOOK ISBN: 978-1-5326-5041-3

Manufactured in the U.S.A.   02/12/18

Contents

Acknowledgements

I AM GRATEFUL FOR the obvious people who have been important to me: my parents (John and Edna Nickel), my husband (Richard Friesen), my children (Melissa and Joanna), and my many friends along the way.

I remember, with thanksgiving, seminary professors, pastoral colleagues, and denominational executives who affirmed my leadership and, sometimes, complicated my journey. It clarified my vocational decisions.

I write this memoir in the luxury of retirement, freed from daily pressures and weekly responsibilities. This reflection time is precious—full of rich experiences, deep delight, genuine confession for mistakes, and daily encouragement to women, especially, to pursue pastoral ministry.

Introduction

THERE ARE TWO QUESTIONS that I get asked the most: "What do pastors really do?" and "What's it like to be a woman pastor?"

The reality is that people often only see their pastors/priests on Sunday for about an hour. They observe preaching (mostly), praying, and then shaking hands at the close of the service. Yes, there are the rituals of baptism, communion, marrying, and burying. Yet, it is those public worship services that occur Sunday after Sunday that give lasting impressions of the up-front acts of leadership. Unless one has a crisis (such as death) or is elected to a major leadership role in the congregation, there may be precious little pastoral contact with most members—especially within a large congregation. And, from my nearly forty years of experience in congregational and denominational leadership positions, it is hard to convey the 24/7 nature of pastoral work.

I could share my datebook filled with committee meetings, staff consultations, phone calls, agendas, minutes, study and sermon preparation, research, appointments with those seeking advice, hospital visitations, continuing education events, contacts with building contractors, and building repair schedules. But those tasks would mask the complex relationships that shaped the living organism called the church.

So, the simple answer I often give when asked what I really do as pastor is something like this: "Let me tell you about my week. . . ." And I recite the conversations with a grieving widow, the evening meeting with the Church Council, the weekly staff meeting, the daily planning for upcoming Sunday worship, the hours spent in the library or researching for the sermon, the tending of the college student wanting to reserve the sanctuary for a wedding a year away, and the rehearsal with scripture readers. I often end my commentary with this caveat: "I love being a pastor because it's just so interesting. Actually, you wouldn't believe what things I deal with!"

Hence, this collection of stories from pastoral ministry.

The second question deals with the complicated life of a female pastor—especially in the Mennonite Church. "Your church deals with disaster relief! You Mennonites send food and aid to countries in war-torn situations! Your congregation quietly serves in volunteer positions in communities. I didn't know that Mennonites ordained women! You don't even look like a Mennonite!"

As a female pioneer of contemporary public positions in the Mennonite world, I have often wandered into leadership by saying "yes" when given the opportunity to serve. I was invited as a college student, for example, to be a secretary (yes, I could type) for a denominational executive and found that church bureaucracy fit me like a glove. I was prepared for pastoring by first teaching for nearly a decade in public and nonprofit schools. I studied and gravitated to higher education easily—loving both the learning and the creativity that seminary and graduate school required. I was born an extrovert but also honed the discipline of listening purposefully. I risked crossing boundaries of female discrimination—saying "yes" to pastoral positions and Mennonite institutional jobs that fit me and beckoned me.

I did not often, in retrospect, think of the vocation of pastoring as mine some four decades ago. I simply could not see why femaleness was a restriction to answering the call to follow Jesus—the Ultimate Boundary-Crosser. Now, it seems, pastoral ministry was my calling to sometimes being the "first" woman or "only" woman in the Mennonite world of ordained leadership.

Hence, this is a volume of stories where gender and pastoral ministry find congruence (and friction). These stories are based on true events but are not entirely factual. Often, names have been changed to protect identities and confidentiality.

Rev. Dorothy Nickel Friesen
Newton, KS; November 2017

CHAPTER 1

Formation

Dangerous Women—"They look harmless, these pioneers of the Women's Movement. But they fought with the deadliest weapon in the world—the invulnerable idea. What these young women carried in their heads was more terrifying to their own generation than the shocking things they said and did. Now the world takes votes and jobs and education for women as commonplaces—things these early fighters were ridiculed for demanding. They spent their lives earning us a legacy of freedom!"

McCall's Magazine, October 1920, p. 16

Perspective

My story begins with an uneventful childhood in Minnesota, as the daughter of farmers in a small town that was about 60 percent Mennonite, 40 percent Lutheran. I was raised in the General Conference Mennonite Church (GCMC) and the Bethel Mennonite Church of Mountain Lake, Minnesota. I joined a huge baby boom of friends who formed a formidable group and, looking back, we were assertive leaders. We were strong, we were smart, and we were given every advantage to use our skills and talents. And many of us girls were tall. I was only slightly shorter than Bev, Susan, Elaine, and Barb but still could manage the front row of volleyball or back row in choir with no problem. From piano lessons to youth group leadership, from school club officers to challenging course work, my classmates and I were expected to achieve—and we did!

I played clarinet and bass clarinet in the band and managed to be selected for the halftime show of a Vikings football game. I carried my bass clarinet on the bus to the Twin Cities, a lonely but exciting ride. Being a leader, it seemed, meant moments of outstanding opportunity and extreme loneliness at the same time.

I was surprised when my cousin, and bus seatmate, and I were called to the principal's office in late May of 1965 to learn that I was valedictorian and she was salutatorian of our class. She knew Latin; I had skipped physics for a class in creative writing! The right-brain classes seemed so satisfying, and my left brain was on a path of absorbing knowledge like a sponge.

It was a heady time to be in college following a very successful high school experience. Bethel College (North Newton, KS) provided a rich environment for study, socializing, and significant intellectual and spiritual growth. While the Minnesota farm remained the foundation and anchor for me, it was the college setting that set my spirit to engage everything in sight. I worked in the cafeteria all four years and learned to know hundreds of students from all over the world by their first names. I joined clubs, developed leadership skills, and enjoyed a steady dating life. It was great to be in college, to learn about global issues, and to try my hand at poetry and essay writing. It was even better to find life-long friends as roommates and mod-mates who, to this day, are strong allies in daily living and evolving life challenges.

I was shaped by two major contextual factors during those college years: the war in Vietnam and my first "real" job as a secretary at the GCMC headquarters at 722 Main Street in Newton during my junior year of college. The war drums were beating loud and long in the late sixties, and the young men around me were in draft lotteries and making life-defining decisions. Pacifism, my internal conviction, was tested with protest marches and public demonstrations. War, it seemed, was eternally sinful and practically stupid.

In that cafeteria of daily work and learning, I found friends and a life partner. He shared my values and seemingly the "right stuff." He was brilliant (smarter than me was a qualification for "spousedom"); he was a leader and capable of challenge (another mark met); and he was from California (that seemed dramatic to me!). And so, after watching him extinguish the love flame of another young woman, we agreed that walking together would suit us both very much. And it has been just so.

The job at "722" came to me from Marv Dirks, then youth director for the GCMC, who was busy planning for the 1968 Mennonite Youth Convention in Estes Park. I was hired in the spring to be a part-time secretary for the Board of Education. I spent hours typing, in triplicate, correspondence for the executive secretary, Willard Claassen, and sitting in on planning meetings for the Youth Convention. I was swept into church programming, church leader meetings, and church bureaucratic organization with ease. The work of the church fit like a nice glove.

The story of my life, then, is a blend of farm and city, local and global, leadership and opportunity, politics and spirituality. Being a woman made all the difference in the world—and still does. I entered the world of church politics and politics entered me.

Orlando's Feet

I'm sure my starched white collar itched a bit as I adjusted my blue choir robe to sing that Sunday morning in the Junior Choir. We lined up in the church parlor, a large basement room with huge wall closets that held both our small, child-sized robes and the large, adult-sized choir robes. We quickly donned our robes, lined up for a final run-through of our morning anthem, and then proceeded through the back hallway, circled through a pastor's study, and finally entered the raised choir loft nestled below beautiful stained-glass windows—all blue, red, and gold in an abstract design.

Since I was a taller girl, I was in the back row and often seated right behind the organ console centered in the tiered loft. We sixth grade girls were a strong bunch who matured early and managed our positions of height with both pride and honor.

The congregation of nearly five hundred was hushed as we followed each other into our assigned row and remained standing to sing the choral call to worship—a carefully chosen (but short) song for that morning. "Do not twitch" would rattle through my childish head as we stood at quiet attention. The "real" pastor then prayed at the "big" pulpit in the center of the sanctuary stage immediately in front of us. Reverence, quietness, and listening were expected. Worship had begun. Then, my favorite part happened.

Rev. Orlando Schmidt was at the organ, and he fingered out an introduction to the opening hymn. I held the blue hymnbook and turned to the appropriate number listed in the bulletin, but my eyes never left the back of the organist. He was masterfully using both hands and both feet as he led the congregation in the majestic hymns, "Holy, Holy, Holy" and "Joyful, Joyful, We Adore Thee." The great hymns of the church were beginning their imprint on my youthful mind. Of course, we sang ALL the verses. Of course, we often sang an "Amen" at the end of the hymn. Of course, we followed the organ's leadership—its pace, its rhythm, its intensity. Sometimes, the final verse was "fancy" with the organ playing more than the typical printed notes.

I saw his feet move back and forth on long wooden pedals, fingers pulling stops on the left and the right. Two keyboards with shiny ivory and black keys and a full array of music pieces were lined up in front of his face on the music stand. It was a miraculous thing to see his whole body perform music. I loved the sound. I loved the words on the pages morphing into people standing together singing. Now, on Sunday morning, what we had practiced earlier came alive. Wow!

Those of us in junior choir (grades 5–8) practiced Wednesday evenings with our assistant pastor, Orlando Schmidt. We sat in a large fellowship hall on cold folding chairs for forty-five minutes with our black folders holding sheet music. I liked feeling a part of a choir and began to get the impression that getting older meant joining the "big" adult choir for Sunday worship. We were gently being led in the church music, which was so different from the music I was learning in piano lessons. I could play tunes from John Thompson's graded piano books like "Home on the Range" and "Indian Drum Song." My piano teachers, from second grade on, also pointed to a hymn for the week.

"What a Friend We Have in Jesus" was an early selection by my great aunt Elizabeth, who was my first piano teacher and a stickler for rhythm and feeling. She instructed in theory, scales, and tunes. But she always included one hymn each weekly lesson. I listened to her wax on and on about the "movement" of the hymn and the "feeling" of the words. Whatever! I was too young to know that notes meant something, and that text provided depth. I was too immature to receive critique for style, exactness, and movement. Whatever!

I practiced faithfully. By junior high, I could play the piano well enough to accompany the kids who met for morning singing before Sunday school lessons. We met in the basement of the nurses' residence across the alley from Bethel Mennonite Church. I sat on a round, adjustable piano stool as I plunked out the introduction on an old, upright mahogany piano. I practiced "Come Thou Almighty King" until my fingers hurt. I learned songs from the "red" junior hymnal. The incorporation of hymnody into a child's piano lessons left long-lasting associations between mind and soul, between body and voice.

The Sunday morning ritual of worship was a habit. We never missed a Sunday. My parents saw to it that the nearly eight-mile farm drive would happen so that I could be in Wednesday night town church activities, which, for our congregation, meant being part of junior choir. I watched the leaders of Sunday school, and I learned from strong men who were preachers and pastors. Rev. Orlando Schmidt, a kind man with reddish hair and a gentle voice, was a welcoming spirit. He was an organist, a musician—not a preacher. I learned that music was part of congregational life and that the organ (and grand piano) were part of how church was done. I learned that men could lead all ages—even children. I fell in love with organ music.

But it was Rev. Schmidt's feet that amazed me. Just how do you play with your whole body? How can you look at all those notes? How did Bach and Beethoven write thousands of notes that looked so complicated on the sheet music? And how could Rev. Schmidt get his feet and his hands to work together? Amazing!

Surely, as a child who was being shaped for future ministry, I was also absorbing hymnody and choral traditions. I was practicing ritual. I was listening to words in preaching and praying. I was integrating sound from voice and instrument. In fact, I was being formed in the Christian tradition for leadership. I also saw the necessity for practice, for repetition, for the routine of exercises like boring scales, and then, finally, the Sunday worship experience. Who knew that Rev. Schmidt's feet would be the symbol of individual talent and corporate product! Who knew that the Holy Spirit's genius lay in the early childhood experiences of observation and sitting in the back row of a junior choir!

Swimming Upstream—The Beginning

The professional life as a woman pastor in the Mennonite denomination can be marked by different eras. While there is a woman named Ann Jemima Allebach, who was ordained at First Mennonite Church of Philadelphia on January 15, 1911, that was done without conference support and she was never assigned a Mennonite congregation. That very early era was followed by years of more traditional roles for women in the church: overseas missionary, pastor's wife, and Sunday school teacher. In many congregations in the United States, women received the right to vote in the 1940s and some became deacons in the 1960s.

However, it wasn't until 1973 when Emma Richards was ordained to serve as co-pastor with her husband, Joe, by the Illinois Conference (Mennonite Church) or 1976 when Marilyn Kauffman Miller was ordained to co-pastor with Peter Ediger at Arvada, Colorado, by the Western District Conference (GCMC) that the twentieth century recognized the entry of women into pastoral ministry.

In many cases, these early pulpit pioneers were second-career women, as was I. My first love and professional vocation was teaching. It never crossed my mind to lead a congregation, preach, or guide an area conference as its minister. My earliest memory of church leadership was the youth group of my congregation (Bethel Mennonite Church, Mountain Lake, Minnesota) in the early 1960s.

It was a typical summer weekend retreat for the senior high youth group executive. (Yes, we used that term.) As a junior in high school, I was elected as secretary to a leadership team. For the retreat, we met at a cabin at nearby Lake Shetek State Park. The speaker was an African American from Chicago! (Much later, I learned that Ed Riddick, our speaker, was part of the Rainbow Coalition with Jesse Jackson in the Chicago civil rights movement.) To this day, I have no idea how this invitation was secured, but it may have been connected to the Fresh Air project, which was part of our congregation's summer program. Kids from Chicago (often black) came to live with a white family in rural Minnesota for a period of time. No doubt, our speaker accompanied these students.

In any case, it was not a fun weekend. It rained and rained. We were cooped up in the cabin but, miraculously, I was touched by something great. This guest, this energetic "preacher," was a great teacher and animated leader. I remember, vividly, sitting on top of a picnic table we had dragged inside as we crowded around listening to his devotional. "Are you ready to lead?" "Can you follow Jesus wherever that might take you?" In my mind, I was ready to say, "Yes," to that call. He blessed our executive team in the presence of the youth sponsors amidst a messy cabin where open bags of potato chips, boxes of candy bars, and bowls full of oranges and apples lay on couches. The text was from Acts 2. "Are you ready for the Holy Spirit?" And just as sure as day, I felt anointed for leadership in the youth group.

But nothing was as formative that 1964 summer as the historic action by my pastor, Rev. Albert Gaeddert, who took a few weeks' leave from senior pastor duties at my congregation to register new (black) voters in Mississippi. The height of the civil rights era reached our northern, Mennonite, white congregation in a profound way. He came back and preached, per my adolescent ears, a justice Gospel. Skin color meant nothing to God but love. It was up to the people of God to love, accept, and strive for just laws. And so, with teenage bravado, a few of us in the youth group asked to be on the agenda of the deacon's meeting.

Since our congregation was searching for a new associate pastor, why not make an appeal for an African American? We presented our case in a small basement classroom. I remember one deacon, evidently exhausted from his day, kept his eyes shut while we spoke. They listened. All six men were circled around the table. One by one, they responded to our request.

"Thank you for your thoughtful presentation. Of course, you know this will not be possible."

"You have a good idea, but it's not practical for our church."

"Where did you get this idea?"

"We will be praying for the right candidate to come to our church."

"Anything else?"

With that, we were dismissed.

When I got home after having driven the nearly eight miles in the country, I was steaming. I slammed the car door and pushed into the house. My parents, seated around the dining room table with newspapers in hand, listened as I shouted, "They aren't Christians! They didn't care a bit about what we said. Didn't they listen to Rev. Gaeddert's sermons? This is the church! It's time to speak up."

And with that, I stomped upstairs to my bedroom.

A little later, I came down the steps, calmer, to attentive but stoic silence and parents in the same chairs. My mother said, "Now calm down. Getting angry won't help." And my dad quietly added, "Not all good things happen quickly."

That was that. No more discussion but no criticism, no discouragement. In fact, no lectures about anything. I figured out that I was right, and they probably agreed with me but couldn't argue with a passionate teenager.

That same summer, I was chosen by the local Veterans for Foreign Wars Auxiliary to be the Minnesota Girls State representative from my high school. (The irony of a pacifist being chosen was curious and probably worrisome for my parents.) This followed the completion of my junior year, and I was facing my last year of high school. I traveled by bus to a Minneapolis college by myself and enjoyed a full week of leadership training. I even ran for office. After all, with the name of "Nickel," I surely should be voted the treasurer for the Girls State! "Get your Nickel's worth," was my slogan, and I carefully created posters and signs urging others to vote for me. I campaigned (and lost) in an environment where other females were talented, assertive, and trying their hand at new roles. When I came back to Mountain Lake and did the required presentation at the Auxiliary meeting, one woman, wearing her navy-blue beret, remarked, "You're a good speaker. You should go into politics!"

Little did she know that politics would be the stuff of my pastoral life.

The Pearl Necklace

Several months into my first year in college, I began to note that two men were paying a lot of attention to me. One was a local Kansas boy, also a first-year student, and one a senior from South Dakota. Both were fun to be with. I went to movies, concerts, and events on campus, often with a date. Actually, I think I saw Dr. Zhivago about four times with four different boys. Studying was scheduled, too, so grades would not suffer from the regular dining hall job, the steady dating, and the late-night dorm activities and gabbing. I loved my first semester.

However, it appeared that my South Dakota friend loved me more than I knew. He was a history major on his way to seminary. He was determined to find a wife to take along on his mission to serve the church and his Lord. I didn't really pay much attention to his intentions but enjoyed the assurance that most activities that I wanted to attend also included a date. Football games, a more formal affair as girls wore dresses, were in downtown Newton, so a boy with a car was a great asset. I maneuvered between local-boy and distant-boy with ease. Finally, the South Dakota boy became a more regular companion.

The relationship reached a new level of intensity over Easter break during second semester. He took me home to visit his parents, but then drove me to my home in Minnesota. I innocently thought it was so nice of him to offer a ride home during spring break. But then, in his farm home, his parents gushed over me and told me how much Tom had shared about me.

Later that night, when his parents were in bed and only Tom and I were on the couch watching a late-night TV show, did I find out that he intended romance and future marriage. I was shocked when a necklace with a gold chain and a single pearl appeared from a small box and he carefully put it around my neck. Of course, I was grateful and flattered. Of course, I was smitten with joy and giddiness from this attention and obvious love.

After a few kisses, I disentangled myself from his embraces and shyly went to my bedroom—his sister's. He promised more plans in the morning as we would drive to my home in Minnesota, 125 miles east.

Sleep was a jumbled mess. What was I going to tell my parents? How in the world would I tell Tom that I thought he was a great guy but there was no way that I was ready for a serious relationship, let alone marriage! Oh my God! Things were way out of control.

The visit at home was short and sweet with no conversation about our relationship. Tom stayed for noon dinner, returned to South Dakota, and then I had several days of peace and quiet. It was great to be home. Plans for summer were emerging. I had an opportunity to go to Chicago for the summer and be a nanny. Several of us Bethel girls were signed up, including my roommate. I would earn money—and I would not be near Tom or South Dakota!

The rest of the school year was awkward in that I told Tom I was not ready for marriage and that I intended to date others. We remained friends, but things cooled off. I wore the necklace some of the time.

In the summer, I went to Chicago and was nanny to five children. Several Bethel boys also came to Chicago to drive city bus routes. Mondays were days off for the entire crew of Bethel nannies and bus drivers, so we rendezvoused at museums, concerts, and restaurants. It was exhilarating to taste new foods, see great works of art, navigate the city streets, and learn about families other than my own. The family my roommate nannied for was Jewish. Mine was Catholic, yet we had so many things in common. I cooked and baked, laid by the swimming pool, and ate many, many hotdog lunches. My five kids were ages six through fifteen, so games, art projects, and country club routines filled most days. And, of course, there was the flirting and attention from other Bethel boys.

I got a letter one day from Tom in mid-summer. He was coming to visit that next weekend and had a surprise for me. He even called, and I gallantly tried to discourage a visit. "No need to drive all that way. We can talk by phone," I suggested. "No, no," he insisted. "I'm eager to see you." And so it was.

The Saturday night date with Tom was a dinner and long conversation. Things were cordial, but I knew in my heart I had to tell the truth. He was going to seminary and was on a high from graduating from Bethel College with distinction. After telling me he was so excited about graduate school, he said, "You have to come with me. There are lots of colleges in Indiana.

You'd be a great pastor's wife. You're smart and social. You can cook and take care of kids. You even play the piano! You're just perfect for me."

That night, I slept little due to both an aching heart and an aching back, which had bothered me from time to time since eighth grade when I slid into second base playing softball. I was NOT ready for marriage, and I was not going to quit Bethel College. It was agonizing.

The next morning was Sunday, and he picked me up for a breakfast at a restaurant. After pancakes, he reached into his pocket and produced a small box. The surprise was a pearl ring that matched the necklace, which I wore all that weekend. I took his hands in mine, looked him right in the eyes, and said, "Tom, you're a great guy, but I am not going to marry you. I'm going back to Bethel in the fall and I intend to graduate. I am not ready for marriage to you or anyone." With that, I put the ring back in the box, took off the necklace, put it on top of the ring, closed the box, and gave it back to him. "You are a good friend, and I thank you for this wonderful relationship. It was a surprise to me how you could think about me as your wife. There will be someone else some day for you and for me."

He let go of me and we said very little. The drive back to my summer home was quiet. We kissed a brief goodbye, and I went inside as he drove off. It was over. I never looked back.

Wasting Time

I wanted counsel and direction for the next academic year. Where should I put my academic energies? Should I continue as a seminary student? What courses should I take? Should I continue in the Master of Religious Education track—the typical female route—or should I switch to the Master of Divinity (MDiv)—often leading to ordination? Was I destined to be the Sunday school teacher or the pulpit preacher? My kindly, rotund advisor was a trusted professor, a leader in the world of Mennonite organizations, a writer of curriculum, an advocate for Christian education. He was respected. I had followed his advice as I switched from "audit" to "credit" in order to continue my teaching vocation. I was leaving behind a "help-meet" role ever so gently. However, crossing the boundary to pastoral leadership seemed foolhardy at best, impossible at worst.

"Go back to teaching," my Mennonite seminary advisor recommended. "You are obviously a good student, but what would you do with a seminary degree? There aren't any church jobs for you and, besides, it's not good that you are wasting professors' time that could be directed toward future pastors." And with that, I exited his office and determined to leave seminary. The year was spring 1974.

Leaving seminary after three years was common—for degree completers—so our male classmates were interviewing and finding jobs across Canada and the United States. We, on the other hand, were shifting in focus. Spouse Richard was now a degree-candidate in the newly minted Master of Peace Studies program. He felt less and less suited for the MDiv and less and less called to be a pastor—however valued that was.

We joined a "panic" group— with four other couples who were critical of the church as an institution and also doubted their suitability for the pastorate. Aptly named the "Non-Pulpit Bounders," we met weekly and encouraged each man to complete their degrees but seek other avenues of Christian service. One couple returned to social work; one couple was hired by the General Conference Mennonite Church in the department of peace and justice; one couple returned to Canada to work on Mennonite history projects; one couple went to a PhD religion program. Ironically, all five of the couples remained deeply involved in the Mennonite denomination, and eventually four men and one woman (me) later served as ordained pastors! When Richard graduated and we needed income, we decided on community-based service jobs in Kansas.

I was leaving behind advocacy for women to study in seminary. I helped establish the first daycare—finding an apartment on campus that would be freed to house cribs, rocking horses, and building blocks instead of students. We formed a parent cooperative and took turns caring for each other's children.

I had been part of a steering committee to design a new course, "Women in Church and Society," which proved to be highly popular with over thirty students (mostly women) who enrolled in an evening course (another new programmatic option). I read widely in feminist theology and was buoyed by cultural shifts in the United States by women's liberation. I debated a faculty member (John H. Yoder) in front of fellow students one evening. The topic was healthcare for women—including abortion in the case of rape or incest. Yet I never saw these roles as pastoral or institutional. I was simply a Christian, a Mennonite, a baptized woman. Surely those three markers were worthy regardless of role.

We rejected the job opportunity to share the pastorate at Rainbow Boulevard Mennonite Church. Instead, we accepted a part-time community organizer role for Richard and a part-time English teacher role for me in a grant-funded alternative school in the Kansas City, Kansas, neighborhood of Rosedale. Both positions were ecumenical in their organizations and dedicated to issues of justice. We would job share and alternate child care for our toddler daughter. With a joint salary offer of $6,600 and no benefits, we moved to hot Kansas in June of 1974.

Seminary studies for me were over—for now.

CHAPTER 2

Decision

"Generally, women who hoped to be ordained to the ministry in the last century faced a lonely struggle, even with a sympathetic denomination. The decision to ordain women has always been a struggle, a deeply divisive and highly emotional discussion. No wonder women who sense a call to serve the church (as pastors) gulp. No wonder that young girls may still never see a woman in the pulpit in their home congregations. When the pastor wears a skirt, there is bound to be controversy."

Dorothy Nickel Friesen, Bluffton University Forum address,
Bluffton, OH; November 14, 2006

Complicated Vocation

Things got complicated. I taught English until the alternative school lost its funding in the spring of 1976—just as I gave birth to our second daughter and decided that I needed a master's degree to stay in teaching. I began graduate studies in summer school and managed mothering two young children, academic work, volunteer church work, and sharing household duties.

It was in the following fall semester that one of my professors mentioned that a local public-school district had a mid-year high school English position opening. The job description specifically mentioned dealing with "challenging, low-performing students." I applied and got the job! I began teaching the week before Christmas. Babysitting for our baby daughter worked out; our older daughter went to pre-school; Spouse Richard dropped to part-time work; I became a full-time teacher. This was my joy.

Meanwhile, I was a volunteer in our Mennonite church. I was on committees and task forces, and I was a committed member of the Friday night potlucks of folks who all were focused on community justice. Our small group was supportive of our family, as we encouraged each other in various secular jobs. Finally, a theme emerged. "Why don't we form a rural-urban center here in Kansas City? This would be a place for rural folks to come to the city for seminars and service experience." Funding? I asked. Well, that would take some time. "How about you go to seminary here in KC, finish your MDiv, and become the director? We have two years to find funding."

Early in 1982, I resigned from a teaching position in Kansas City, Kansas, with the Turner School District. It was a hard decision. I loved teaching. I had completed the MA in Religion and Education with a focus on teaching the Bible as literature to low-performing students. But year after year, I was "Mrs. Friesen in Room 235." The challenge was missing. I created innovative reading programs that had become a natural part of the curriculum. I was the department chair to thirteen teachers—all who were cooperative, professional, and effective. Yet, something nagged within me. Is this all there is?

And so, I resigned from teaching, packed up my hundreds of files and books, and enrolled at St. Paul School of Theology, a United Methodist seminary. I was accepted with a generous scholarship, and Rainbow Mennonite Church employed me as a pastoral intern on a part-time basis ($500 per month) while I was a student. I was no longer a teacher. I was making a vocational shift—an exciting but daunting challenge. Yet, I never thought of myself as a pastor. I was engaging the system of the church as I was rejecting the system of public education. I maintained my teaching files, notes, and books until 1990 when I, tearfully, did not renew my teaching certificate. I sat on the floor of our attic amidst boxes belonging to Mrs. Friesen, tossing many worksheets and class notes into the garbage bag and filling the recycling box with most of the remaining files. It was then that I knew I was embracing a new identity.

The ministerial credential for pastoring and leading a congregation didn't really occur to me at the beginning of my seminary training. I was fully aware of the controversy in the country regarding the role of women in many occupations and the huge conflicts in the Mennonite church about ordaining women. I took every opportunity that was offered to me to serve on church-related committees and task forces including some denominational ones. I believed that my baptism was valid and necessary for leadership and that my gender was incidental to that call. Obviously, others did not share my view. Seminary education afforded me the luxury to study, attend conferences, and delve into scholarship regarding the role of women in religion. My library of books grew by the hundreds. I was supportive of women doing theology, teaching at all levels, and leading as they were gifted for any position in the church.

I was licensed toward ordination by the Western District Conference of the GCMC and the South Central Conference of the Mennonite Church (MC) because the Rainbow congregation was affiliated with both denominations. It was a complicated time. I prepared documents and my congregation sent supporting statements. I was interviewed by the Western District Conference Ministerial Committee where my gender was *the* issue. Several wondered out loud if I was qualified for the credential since I had not actually graduated from seminary. (It would happen in the next months.) One member firmly stated that this interview was not biblical, and he would vote against me. I was licensed toward ordination and graduated from seminary in May 1984.

Yet, I didn't identify as a pastor. I was simply getting the credential needed to work with other denominations in forming new urban ventures and organizing our congregation for community justice ministries. I wandered into pastoral leadership through doors that cracked open in nontraditional ways.

The trajectory of an urban institute fell apart. Now what? A kindly conference minister had strongly encouraged me to fill out the Ministerial Leadership Information (MLI) form. I did, but I thought it would be perfunctory. I was graduating; I did not have a job; I was a newly minted seminary graduate. What the heck! Fill out the form! And, remarkably, the essay questions were deep and thorough, and my pen flew across the page. Answers and thoughts jelled quickly, and the multi-paged MLI was finished in a matter of hours. Was this a sign of pastoral leadership? No, I was still caught up in a teacher-in-the-city-who-does-interesting-things identity.

Then my life took a decisive and dramatic turn. That MLI led to an interview for a pastoral position in Manhattan, Kansas—one hundred miles west of KC. I interviewed there, but, despite all my criteria for ministry (inter-Mennonite, non-traditional, no building to maintain, small, justice-oriented, a good fit for our family) being affirmed, I used the familiar excuses to turn down the initial call to another city. "I can't move our family." "What would my spouse do?" "We love our current congregation and don't want to leave." "I'm not sure I'm ready to lead a congregation." I said "no" to their first call to serve as solo pastor.

During the summer, their second candidate choice turned them down and they came back to me. I said "yes" this time.

Things were approved—but there was another complication: that congregation was affiliated with three regional Mennonite bodies—not just two! It was a new wrinkle. Now the Mennonite Brethren Church (MB) entered the picture since the GCMC (WDC), MC (South Central), and MB (Southern District) had birthed the Manhattan Mennonite Fellowship as a church plant in 1976. They, too, were part of the pastoral search process. The MB's officially did not (and still do not) call women as lead pastors nor ordain them for that position. However, since the congregation had called and the other two conferences had approved me, the Southern District Conference allowed me to be called as pastor but removed their subsidy from the congregation as a church plant. Poof! There went several thousand dollars because of my gender.

After serving the Manhattan Mennonite Fellowship for months, the congregation requested my ordination. Again, it was complicated. And, again, I was approved by the WDC. The SCC delayed its decision about ordaining me (and another woman that year) until they did a massive survey, held a conference-wide special session, and further processed my call to ministry. In the end, the SCC agreed to ordination.

The Southern District would list me as "Other" in their church directory. The night before the Sunday morning ordination worship service, I received a phone call from a MB pastor and leader who assured me that he approved of my leadership and would be praying for me but could not be present for the service. "I'm sure you understand how complicated this is." I assured him I did.

With lots of relatives, friends, and church leaders from several branches of Mennonites by my side, I was ordained in April 1985. My Kansas City pastor preached a great sermon; the denominational pastors spoke words of scripture and offered official greetings and the official certificate; a graduate student sang a lovely soprano "Alleluia" aria; I knelt, and many hands pressed on my shoulders—including a Catholic nun who wept openly as she stood in the ordaining crowd. We prayed. I stood up a pastor.

I began my journey as a Mennonite pastor with joy and hope—plus a little nervousness. There just might be more complications along the way.

Official Letter

Church
Extension
Evangelism
Commission

PARKSIDE MENNONITE
BRETHREN CHURCH
7143 E. 1'th - PH. 838-8335
TULSA, OKLAHOMA 74112

September 12, 1984

Manhatten Mennonite Fellowship
1221 Thurston
Manhattan, KS 66502

Subject: CEEC FINANCIAL SUPPORT

Dear Brothers and Sisters:

From the conversations and communications you have had with the Church Extension
and Evangelism Commission, you will be aware of some of the basic policies that
guide us as a commission in the Mennonite Brethren Conference. We try to
function under the authority of the Word as understood and defined by the
brotherhood. When a question arises we consult with those who have been given
the responsibility by the conference to guide us in those matters.

As you know, before you brothers and sisters chose your present pastor we
expressed concern. When a CEEC church calls a pastor we want that to be a
joint call. In other words we would like to be in agreement with the call.
When you extended a call to Dorothy Friesen, we as a Commission questioned the
correctness of giving the office of pastor to a woman in the light of our
understanding of the Word. Since we knew this would cause disagreement, we
took the question to the Faith and Life Commission for consideration.

At a meeting of the Faith and Life Commission on August 23, 1984, they
recommended that we write to the Manhattan Mennonite Fellowship to communicate
the following position. We believe that engaging a woman pastor to lead the
fellowship of the church is at variance with the policy of the General Conference
of Mennonite Brethren Churches. Because of this, the Church Extension and
Evangelism Commission will discontinue financial support for the pastor.

This action by CEEC is not intended to imply an end to your membership in the
Southern District Conference, and we encourage continued fellowship with you
in the conference. We want to continue to seek the truth concerning this
matter on which we disagree. May the Lord bless you and us as we seek His
guidance.

Sincerely,

Sid Harms, Chairman
Church Extension & Evangelism Commission
cc: Roland Reimer, Chairman, Faith & Life Commission; William Johnson, Conference
Office Coordinator

Jesus said. "I will build my church...
What is your part in planting a Mennonite Brethren Church?

Bathroom Plot

We were huddled in the women's bathroom at a Mennonite bi-national conference session. I held a file folder with notes from a workshop I had just led called "Women and Theology." The intensity of the small group of us, all full of women's energy for inclusion, was focused on the denomination's business meeting about to start in the large conference room.

"Do you know what's happening next?" one woman asked me as I glanced at the program booklet.

"Well, let's see," I replied. I turned to the appropriate page. "It looks like they will introduce the people on the leadership ballot, so we have time to make our voting decisions in a couple of days."

One woman peered over my shoulder and announced with anger, "Look at the ballot! There are four boards that have no women candidates. It's all men! The delegates are going to vote for new people for the major boards of the General Conference Mennonite Church. We have to do something!"

And with that, we looked around and identified right there at the bathroom sink at least one woman—a college professor with overseas mission experience—who was qualified to be on the "Mission Board."

"Can we nominate you for the ballot?" And without hesitation, she said, "Yes. I doubt if I'll get elected, but I'll be glad to have my name there."

With that, our bathroom plot became a plan. Over the next two days, I was part of a strategy to convince qualified women to allow their names to be nominated from the floor for the various boards. We were ready with four names—including a young law student attending her first denominational conference session. She was assured she would not get elected. "This is symbolic. We just have to get the attention of the delegates."

"Let's find men to offer the nominations," another feminist suggested. Ah, yes, we needed to be strategic in more ways than one. Yes, we had very qualified women in attendance who were ready to stand up and be recognized as a candidate for office. And yes, we had supportive men who would publicly give voice to a female nomination.

The plot was in place.

Two days later, the nominations from the floor included the four women. And all four were elected! The bathroom plot had worked perfectly—and surprisingly successfully.

I met another co-conspirator in the bathroom following the election session. We hugged each other, and I said, "Not bad work! I guess we just have to keep working the system, and someday there will be new voices in leadership."

P.S. This election happened in Estes Park, Colorado, in the summer of 1980. It should be noted, however, that the policy for future triennial conference sessions of the GCMC would forbid nominations from the floor. A vetting system would be put in place with promises of more women being considered for a ballot.

In 1983, my name was on the ballot for a six-year position on the Commission on Home Ministries. I was elected and served on the Executive Committee as chairperson from 1986 to 1989.

Dangerous Pastor

I was the pastor of Manhattan Mennonite Church in Manhattan, Kansas, from 1984 to 1990. This congregation averaged about seventy-five to one hundred people on a Sunday morning. Manhattan is a university town with Kansas State University—a university of then twenty-five thousand students—dominating the scene. Consequently, our congregation featured both graduate and undergraduate students, staff, faculty, and folks associated with the university. It was a creative and loving congregation, prone to recreating itself each fall as new students arrived, graduates departed, and the casual passerby stopped in when they heard singing coming from the campus ministry building where our congregation met for Sunday morning worship.

One September Sunday morning, I, as pastor, was scurrying around putting bulletins on chairs, arranging the worship center, and getting materials out for display when a new young couple arrived—at least twenty minutes early. The assigned greeters at the front door were not in place yet, so I welcomed the couple, invited them to the worship space with a wave of my hand, and handed them the morning bulletin as they quietly moved toward back row chairs.

Naturally, others arrived, and the chairs filled up. The greeters were on duty, the children were running around, the pianist began the prelude, and I assumed my customary seat in the front row with my family—two daughters and husband. The service proceeded; I preached, we sang and prayed, and then I pronounced the benediction. As I went to the exit door to greet those leaving the service, this young couple came to shake my hand.

They looked friendly but reserved. As I shook Stanley's hand, he said something like this:

"We're new in Manhattan. We came because I'll be a graduate student in physics. We're from Delaware and we're Mennonite. We simply looked into the telephone book to see if there was a Mennonite church and we showed up. When you greeted us at the door this morning, we were pleased to find a friendly face. However, when you stood up to preach, our mouths nearly dropped open. You see, we are opposed to having a woman as pastor and had we known that this church allowed it, we would have never come."

I struggled a bit for words and must have said something like, "Well, I hope that you found the service and preaching helpful. You are welcome here anytime."

Stanley responded, "You know, the sermon wasn't that bad. I'm going home to study that passage."

I responded, "Great. Maybe we can have lunch this week. I always eat in the student union on Tuesday. Look for me in the back of the center section. Students and faculty join me, and we would be glad to have you join us."

"Well," said Stanley, "I'm not sure."

That Sunday's attendance turned into many Sundays as Stanley and Martha came faithfully. While they made it abundantly clear that they disapproved of my ministry, they could see that the congregation had, in fact, called me to serve in that role. They believed that communities of faith had that responsibility, and so their own theology did not allow them to leave.

Their attendance spanned nearly two years. When Martha became pregnant, the congregation hosted a baby shower for them. We were all in great excitement as the due date drew near. I received a call from Stanley at the hospital. Martha was in labor and things were not going so well. Would I come to the hospital for prayer?

Of course I would, and I hurried to Martha's side. Stanley stood on one side of the bed, holding Martha's hand, and I stood on the other side. The doctor was performing painful examinations, and Martha was nearly exhausted from many hours of labor for what was clearly a very large baby. I calmly spoke, prayed, and stayed by her side while decisions were being made about her care. Amid many words of thanksgiving for my presence, I stepped aside as she was wheeled into surgery and then stayed at the hospital until a healthy baby boy was delivered. I embraced Stanley, prayed a prayer of thanksgiving, and left for home.

Later that fall, I officiated when we dedicated that precious child and his parents in a worship service. I completely forgot about that initial resistance to my presence as a pastor-who-wears-a-skirt to this young couple.

However, about three months later, the couple invited me to their apartment. In a brief and awkward conversation, they informed me that although I was a fine pastor, and although the congregation was certainly supportive of my ministry, and although I had been important to them in their lives and particularly in the stressful moment of childbirth, they believed they could not raise their son in a congregation where a woman was pastor. They were leaving our congregation for another in our community—not Mennonite and with male leadership—and they did.

My heart still aches as I remember going to the car after that visit, sitting in the parking lot, and crying, "God, how can you call me, gift me, and reward me with a congregation only to have me face rejection? This is too hard. This is not right."

But my tears dried, my life resumed, and I survived rejection—an integral part of my pastoral identity.

Matthew's Confession

Our university congregation had many young children. One particularly sensitive fourth grade boy, Matthew, came back from visiting his grandparents at Christmas vacation time. His grandparents lived in a small, south central Kansas town and attended a Mennonite congregation there. Matthew, of course, had accompanied his grandparents to their worship service—which happened repeatedly during those two weeks, as there had been many special services during the Christmas season.

The first Sunday back at Manhattan, this precocious ten-year-old took me aside and said something like this: "Dorothy, I just have to talk with you."

Sensing some urgency and intensity, I guided Matthew to a corner away from the milling congregation to have a more one-on-one conversation. "So, what's up, Matthew?" I queried.

"Well, Dorothy, I know you're not going to believe this, but I found out something about my grandma's church that's really odd."

Now I was curious. I knew the congregation—a modest, average, traditional, mostly rural-based congregation in the wheat fields of Kansas. What could be "really odd"?

"Well, I just wanted you to know, that church has a *man* for a minister. Isn't that odd?"

Trying hard not to laugh nor belittle this obviously sincere and supportive young parishioner, I gently reassured Matthew that men can be ministers, too.

I remember this story with a deep sense of affirmation and love—also an integral part of my pastoral identity.

Summer Heat

The room was hot even though the air-conditioner was pumping full blast. All twenty or so of us seminary faculty were seated at tables arranged in a large rectangle with files and policy notebooks open in front of us. I was in my second year as an administrative faculty member and responsible for the proposals to admit students into the Master of Divinity program of study. Anyone admitted to the seminary could take classes, but entering a degree track required discernment, documentation, and a recommendation that came from me, the assistant dean.

The applicant was a first-year student. It was during this first year that the student in question entered a relationship with another gay male in the city. I met with the student repeatedly and examined his coursework, his application for the MDiv, and his long-term goals to serve a Mennonite congregation as pastor. There was ample evidence of good grades, Anabaptist/Mennonite theology and values, and a desire for a seminary degree. The complication of being in a gay relationship was not hidden but, of course, was cause for great concern.

"I didn't plan to fall in love!" he blurted out in a conversation months before this meeting. "Do all students pledge to remain single the entire time they are in seminary? Why do I have to be a test case? I am exhausted by this public pressure. But I don't want to leave seminary. I just got started, and I'm sure God wants me to pastor."

This, and other conversations, were heart-wrenching. Variations on the theme meant sleepless nights for him and anxiety for me. I, of course, needed to confide in the academic dean about this "case," and she, too, knew the faculty would be struggling for the right decision regarding Malcolm's application.

The two denominations (General Conference Mennonite Church and Mennonite Church) had been wrestling with issues of human sexuality for well over a decade. A massive process, including a published study guide, had circulated among congregations in the United States and Canada in the early 1980s. Finally, the two denominations passed official statements (GCMC—Saskatoon 1986 and MC—Purdue 1987) that became bedrock decisions for decades to come. The critical sentences stated that "sexual intercourse is reserved for a man and a woman united in marriage" and "this precludes premarital, extramarital, and homosexual activity."

I was at Saskatoon that summer of 1986, a delegate from the congregation I pastored in Kansas. I argued against that particular section of the document, yet I was a full-hearted supporter of the human sexuality discussion process for our church. We needed to wrestle with the many facets of sexuality, which included roles of men and women, incest, abuse, pornography, divorce, and many other topics. These topics were nearly obliterated by the tense and vigorous floor debate on the section about homosexuality. I sat beside a lesbian who was quietly weeping as vicious things were said about homosexual persons at the open-mic sharing in delegate discussion. I had to vote "no" on adopting the statement even though I agreed with virtually all other sections of the motion.

Of course, I could not have anticipated that six years later this very document would be the crux of the argument for denying a student admission to a degree program at a Mennonite seminary. By then, I had resigned my pastorate to move to Elkhart, Indiana, and I used my pastoral experience to present my recommendation for Malcolm.

The faculty, overheated in many ways, proceeded to vote. "All those voting 'yes' to deny Malcolm admission to the MDiv plan of study, raise your hand." Every hand but mine went up.

"All those who vote 'no' on this motion, raise your hand."

I voted "no."

Malcolm came to my office later. "I'm leaving Elkhart," he declared. "I cannot stay here much longer. Brad and I must work out our relationship somehow. Thanks for all you have done. I knew it wasn't going to turn out well."

With that, the tension within the faculty, the seminary constituency, and the denomination kept near a boiling point—for the next thirty years.

Pastoral Scars

In my role as the only female clergy in the Ministerial Association in the mid-1980s, I often was asked, "Well, how's it going? Are they being nice to you?" I thought it odd, since I enjoyed respect and authority from my congregation.

Then, one of the senior pastors from a large local congregation invited me to lunch. He said he wanted to welcome me to the city, give me some inside tips on the town, and discuss theology. I was ready for support and non-Mennonite affirmation. However, the lunch turned quickly to another agenda. He began to describe a "secret" arrangement where he and I would meet to talk about the latest issues in theology. He "loved" my mind and didn't see any other clergy as bright as me. Immediately, the lunch salad became impossible to eat. The tea needed more ice. I was trapped in a restaurant date that became altogether uncomfortable. "You and I could become special friends," he projected. "See," he said, "the Mennonites were smart and brought you to me. We will be a great theological team." Shocked, I thanked him for lunch and never met with him alone again.

I don't think I ever thought of pastors, teachers, or authority leaders as dangerous. I accepted them as responsible, necessary, and helpful. I respected my elders, my parents, and my relatives. I was oblivious to issues of incest, abuse, and sexualized violence. Those dangers were, quite simply, not in my world as a young woman.

After I was married and then pastoring years later, I received a call from a friend who informed me that one of my former pastors had been dismissed from a Mennonite agency because of his infidelity to his wife. He had, by accounts, been flirtatious with other women, attempted to seduce them, and functioned as a predator with young women. "Why didn't he just keep his pants zipped!" chirped my colleague. I hung up the phone and said, "I knew something was wrong, but I had no idea what was really going on."

I wondered how I had escaped such attention from him and, upon reflection, how I had also missed intuitive nudges that certain behaviors were secretly happening. I rationalized that it was, after all, the sixties and seventies. Women's liberation was the cultural rage. Friends were getting divorced and family members also experienced marital separations. The "pill" had given us women protection from unwanted pregnancy. Sexual freedom was enticing, and the secular news was filled with "love-ins" and "hippie communes."

My emerging pastoral identity was often surprised by the pre-marital counseling sessions where serious events of rape, multiple sexual partners, and affairs with married men were revealed. I listened to a tearful account of abortion when a seminary-bound woman discovered herself pregnant by a former boyfriend who did not want to marry a potential pastor. Mennonites? Yes, Mennonites.

The pastoral identity of a female in ministry is one that develops both gradually and dramatically. The scars of broken former pastors and the continuing sense of self-care developed and expanded over time. I became more careful, maybe even jaded. I suspected that words of praise might be hidden attempts of seduction and that I would succumb to foolish indiscretion. Each incident of praise became suspect. Each suggestion for "lunch sometime?" needed to be parsed. The tendency to be overly self-critical became hyper.

Looking back, I had been prepared to be a pastor and to guard my boundaries by previous incidents of abuse of power. A former seminary professor had tested my boundaries by putting his hand up my leg while traveling in a car. He was "experimenting" with friendship, he touted, but I felt trapped as he drove the car while I was secured in the passenger seatbelt. That same professor, years later, had held me against the kitchen refrigerator in a long, groping hug as my husband took the babysitter home. Both events were wrong and shocking. It was not safe, it seemed, to be left alone with powerful men.

It's a terrible and important learning to know that identity is shaped by personal ambition, will, and preparation, but that it is also honed by experiences—some positive and some negative. The scars of emotional trauma were just as real as the accolades of admiring colleagues and congregational members.

It became clear to me that women should be listened to and believed. Small incidents of sexualized behavior were often relegated to "not that bad" and shoved deeper into the hidden lives of leaders. The gradual public airing of sexual abuse by Catholic priests was mirrored by every other denomination—including Mennonite.

As a pastor and female leader, my professional life has been marked with being the "only" woman on many committees. I traveled safely with male clergy colleagues for many miles in rental cars to denominational meetings. I was often lonely for my female friends who shared comparable positions. They often confessed in private conversations that they, too, had experienced "odd stuff."

I learned to extend my hand quickly and obviously when greeting men—even though I am a "hugger" and appreciate warm engagement. I learned to avoid offices that had no hallway windows. I arranged furniture in my offices so that I always was closest to the exit and my conversation partner was not blocking my escape if one became necessary. I met with men in public places or in a place where other staff or visitors were present. I advocated for professional training in prevention of clergy abuse and saw to it that every pastor in my area conference had that as part of their resume. And, in the end, I loved pastoring and administration in Mennonite churches and institutions.

My emotional scars became symbols of healing and hope. I had survived disappointment, anger, and disgust from broken pledges and inappropriate actions. I had a husband who trusted me absolutely. I thrived in pastoral and administrative ministry. Yet, I will ever be on my guard to protect my integrity and identity. Pastoral identities and self-awareness go through stages—but woe to any pastor who forgets to understand their authority, their power, and their responsibility.

Liturgical Clothing Commandments

I. Don't wear a sundress when preaching

Years ago, a summer pastor arrived in my home congregation. He was a Mennonite intern intent on becoming, as I imagined, a "real" pastor. His wife, an attractive woman with striking black hair, came to their first Sunday worship service wearing a spaghetti-strapped sundress. I still remember the white flowing dress with huge red flowers and straps tied neatly on each shoulder. I had never seen such a dress in my congregation—certainly not on a pastor's wife and absolutely not in the second pew from the front! At dinner following church, my mother kindly noted, "She's from the South where it's much warmer than here in Minnesota." That shrewd comment from my own mother was a rare critique of church leadership and their judgements.

Now, after thirty-five years of public Mennonite ministry, I don't wear a sundress when preaching—even in hot Kansas. When a pastor wears a skirt, there are already huge barriers to overcome: resistance to women preachers, comments about clothing rather than sermon content, and the dilemmas about apparel. These are all barriers that men probably don't have.

II. Wear seasonal colors to fit the liturgical calendar

I wore purple in Advent and Lent, white on Easter and Christmas, and red for Pentecost and Reformation Sunday. The bright gold jacket was reserved for Epiphany and the black suit for Good Friday. Of course, there were plenty of opportunities to vary colors and designs, but the "holy" days seemed to be ones where my preaching and preparation were enhanced by carefully chosen attire.

The most difficult choices of clothing were reserved for weddings. Not black—too somber; not white—conflicted with the bride; no colors that clashed with bridesmaid's dresses; and nothing dramatic or bold. Navy was often the choice. Modest and muted dresses are part of most wedding portraits where I stand with the beaming bride and groom.

Early in my career, I went to Kansas City to shop for a dress because I had about four summer weddings coming up. I tried on several dresses and finally went to a more formal dress shop. The friendly clerk inquired, "And how can I help you today?" I explained I needed a dress for a wedding, but before I could explain my role, she said, "And what are the bride's colors?" "No, no," I said. "I'm officiating at the wedding. I'm the pastor."

She looked startled and then perplexed. She was quiet and went to one side of the store, then to the other side, and then finally came back to me. "I'm sorry, but we don't have clothes for someone like you."

III. Choose clothes with pockets

Oh yes, the necessity of pockets became a factor. Handkerchiefs and tissues were demanded for my tears that escaped during pastoral prayers or sneezes that erupted because of the floral arrangement directly in front of the pulpit. Sometimes the bride or groom was tearful, and I sneaked a tissue to them. More than likely, I wore jackets with pockets to hold cough drops, tissues, and microphone battery packs because a belt is not a common women's clothing accessory (but generally worn by men). Despite the pocket dress code, even now, decades later, I find tissues stuffed in Bibles and sermon folders!

IV. Beware of dangly earrings

When I chose to have my ears pierced, I deliberately wanted to wear earrings that moved and flowed. However, when I preach, those earrings are modest and generally "less dangly." It's especially wise when officiating at the dedication of infants and children to wear no necklaces and no earrings that children can grab. Holding precious children while balancing microphone cords and a minister's manual is precarious enough, let alone while guarding jewelry. I know. I learned this the hard way when a necklace of (fake) pearls spilled on the floor with a clatter after a baby accidently caught hold and ripped the strand during the final dedicatory prayer.

V. Wear sensible shoes

On to the feet. I have long since given up high heels—although I loved to wear them with pencil skirts. Now, I'm more confident with a flat shoe or chunky heels. Being firmly grounded is important! Summer in Kansas, especially, means sandals and open-toed comfort shoes. However, for a more public and professional look, I am careful to wear a dressy sandal for Sunday and a more closed-toed shoe for funerals and weddings.

Once, I received a call from a distraught member of a local church. "Since you are the conference minister, can't you do something about the pastor's shoes?"

I was taken aback. Asking for more information, I discovered a female pastor had been the officiant at the funeral and the burial. At the cemetery, as Pastor Suzy led the prayers in blazing heat, the parishioners could not take their eyes off her bright red toenail polish and sparkling sandals.

"It was downright disrespectful," concluded the grieving niece. "My ninety-three-year-old aunt deserved more respect. Do something! These women pastors need to be told what to wear!" And with the plunk of the phone, she hung up.

Yes, at the open grave, bright toenails were a huge distraction. Conservative dress; liberal compassion.

VI. Do not be anxious about what you wear

The role of clothing for women in public office is, and probably should be, a matter of carefulness and appropriateness. Each of us has different tastes and styles—thank goodness. However, if folks remember more about my earrings than the sermon, I probably should reconsider my next jewelry. The medium is the message, and, for women, dress has always been a marker of pastoral authority. From the veiled head to the nun's habit, women have dressed for roles of leadership. While bishops in other traditions can wear flowing robes, we Mennonites have eschewed robes and stoles. I often wish that a simple robe with a stole that matches the season or occasion would be a welcome garb. Maybe in my old age, I'll dress differently—but not with purple hair.

Parallel Threads

Scene 1 (1960s): My mother is sitting at the dining room table working on her agenda for the next meeting of Worship and Sew—our church's younger women's group. (The older women meet in a group called The Mission Society.) Mom is now the "chairman" of the program committee, so she finds speakers and introduces them. Her notebook is filled with notes and telephone numbers, and she is steadfast in attending to details and organization. Worship and Sew, which we kids nicknamed "Gossip and Sew," is an important leadership opportunity for women.

Scene 2 (1980s): Twenty years later, I decide to enter a United Methodist seminary to complete my Master of Divinity which I started a decade earlier at the Mennonite seminary in Elkhart, Indiana but never finished. I look for scholarships and fill out aid forms. Unfortunately, no Mennonite groups—women's, ministerial, conference, or denominational—will give financial aid to a Mennonite woman attending a non-Mennonite seminary. I am employed on a part-time basis in a Mennonite church with every intention of being a Mennonite upon completion of my degree. Fortunately, the United Methodist women's organization of that region awards me a very generous scholarship that funds nearly all my tuition for one year—even though I have no intention of serving in a United Methodist congregation.

Scene 3 (1980s): My mother reports that the two women's groups have combined into one group now renamed "Women in Mission." There simply are too few women in the older group, so they cannot maintain their program and energy or find women who will lead. "What is the future of our group?"

Scene 4 (1980s): I am licensed and then ordained for ministry by the Western District Conference and South Central Conference of (now) Mennonite Church USA. This involves a complicated path as the ordination of women is highly controversial. Multiple study groups, special task forces, and additional area conference sessions are called to test the will of congregations as they call women pastors who are ready to serve. Accusations of "women's lib" fly around. Women who are leading local congregational women's groups are desperate to "keep" women in their organization and waffle in their support of women in ministry. Women pastors band together in support groups and host "Women in Ministry" conferences, and I give much energy to such efforts. I get asked, "Aren't all women in ministry? Why must you have your own group?" Tensions are evident as theological arguments rage throughout the denomination.

Scene 5 (1990s): My mother retires from her job as church secretary (often called administrative assistant in most circles) at her congregation after seventeen years. Her modest pay is a source of great pride, and her soul is satisfied as she is recognized for her important contribution to the congregation's ministry and support of the pastoral staff. She affirms me. She keeps a scrapbook of newspaper clippings where my name appears. She and Dad worry about the stress I experience when others doubt my authority for church leadership. I experience the greatest criticism from other women—especially those invested in a local women's group—and from major male leaders of area conferences. My mother continues her steadfast involvement in the Women in Mission group. She tithes and sends scholarship money to the Mennonite seminary.

Scene 6 (1990s and 2000s): I pastor, lead denominational committees, write in Mennonite publications, and speak at national assemblies. I am visible and engaged in Christian leadership based on my baptism vows to serve God with all my heart, soul, and mind. I thrive. It is interesting to navigate the invitations to speak at women's groups in the church, to join the quilting events (I do not know how), to serve at a local wedding reception, and to bring pie to a funeral meal as I also preach, counsel, and lead the Church Council discernment process in delicate and difficult conversations. Just what am I to do with a women's group in the church that offers excellent leadership and caring ministries for women but also siphons off those women from serving as deacons, moderators, area conference leaders, and future seminary students?

Scene 7 (2004): My mother, now 80, says, "I always knew you would be a pastor. I miss going to church and being part of the women's group. I miss serving at the receptions, hosting visiting choirs, and organizing guest speaker programs. What will happen to the women's group? It is so small.

How will we find new leaders? It was so good for me to part of Women in Mission. I guess I will still pray for you and the church."

Scene 8 (today): I give thanks for one hundred years of women in mission—in rural, urban, large, and small congregations. I pray for new leaders. I will mentor women at all ages to share their gifts in the church, in the community, in the world. I will challenge sexism and role-restricting policies that relegate women to positions that perpetuate submissive roles. I will name our church structures that always have women's groups as "affiliate" or "associate" levels as wrong. I will share my money, time, and talent to expand the ministry of Jesus Christ for women, especially, as long as I live.

CHAPTER 3

Love and Death

Weddings and Funerals

"I write on the Plains, in a small town. I am indelibly an outsider, because I write and because I spent my formative years away. I am also an insider by virtue of family connections. I have a unique role here and try to respect its complexity." "...I am entrusted with many stories here, and I have my own to tell. What I often wonder is why the others are not telling theirs."

Kathleen Norris, *Dakota—A Spiritual Geography*, New York: Houghton-Mifflin, 1993, 86–87.

Missing Groom

"Is Tony in there?" I literally shouted into the men's bathroom. I was searching for the groom, who was now missing from the prescribed meeting room
in the large church. (As a woman pastor, I always rehearsed the logistics of
wedding processionals. I couldn't assume that men would be ready to enter
at the right time with me, so I arranged for an exact time and exact place
to gather prior to the procession.) However, at this wedding, when I went
to the anteroom, I saw only a couple of groomsmen in their tuxedoes. The
other three brothers plus the groom were missing.

"Where are the others? And where's the groom?" I had asked just minutes ago.

With sheepish grins, the two said that he was probably in the bathroom and they would go get him. Time was running out.

We were in one of the largest churches in the community, a place that
accommodated a very formal wedding. The wedding party was large. The
bride was a member of a sorority and had five attendants. The groom, with
three brothers and two fraternity members, had his five attendants. The
rehearsal had gone quite smoothly, although the Mennonite bride had tried
to maintain her composure while future brothers-in-law made silly comments and were generally childish. She had secured university professors to
provide the music, and I learned quickly that they had no patience.

"We were supposed to be here only one hour, and you are not on
time," chided the organist at rehearsal. The trumpeter sat near the organ
looking bored and irritated. They had no time for a pastor who seemed to
have trouble handling a dozen twenty-somethings—some with alcohol on
their breath.

Eventually, the rehearsal was over. We made sure everyone was clear
about where to dress for the wedding, how the processional would work,
and how the groom's family would be seated since the parents were divorced
and refused to sit in the same pew. I orchestrated a seating chart that finally

was agreed to by the parents and an equally vocal grandmother. Clearly, the religious act of marriage was overshadowed by shenanigans and partying.

"Why, oh why, do I officiate at weddings?" I muttered under my breath. Weddings, it seemed, were stressful and filled with old customs and myths with bridal magazine demands. Never mind that I was officiating at a religious event. Forget that I would sign a license that guaranteed legal rights. And certainly, disregard the awesome meaning of wedding vows. I hated the role of referee instead of priest.

I yelled again, "Is Tony in there?" With some amount of bravery, I pushed open the bathroom door to find the bathroom empty.

I whirled around and faced the two frat brothers who were laughing. "Where are they? What did you do to him?" I demanded.

I now suspected that the groom had been kidnapped by his three fun-loving brothers.

"Find them now!" I demanded.

I looked at my watch. The organist was supposed to start the processional, and the bridesmaids were, no doubt, beginning their long walk from the adjoining education wing of the church to the sanctuary. Timing was everything!

I ran in dress heels, bounded two by two up the stairs to the back of the sanctuary from the basement, and told the ushers to deliver a note to the organist: "missing groom, keep playing." The ushers complied, and the service was delayed. Then I told the approaching bridesmaids to stop walking as I saw them in their shimmering purple gowns getting too close to the sanctuary. "Stop. I'll let you know when to walk in. Don't move."

With that, I raced down the stairs and witnessed the two frat brothers open an exit door to the parking lot. I followed and saw, with horror, his three brothers in the bed of a pickup truck. They were pulling the groom out of the back and loosening ropes from his feet and a blindfold from his face. They were shouting with laughter and howling as the groom tried to steady himself after being manhandled. He jumped off the back of the pickup, smoothed his tuxedo, and ran toward me.

"So sorry, but these guys were having a little fun. How does my hair look?"

Startled and fuming, I simply said, "Get in here now. You look fine."

With that, I scurried to the back of the church with instructions to the usher to tell the organist to start the processional. I nodded to the bridesmaids they could continue their walk to the back of the sanctuary, and I hastened to the anteroom to meet the groom and his attendants.

With a fifteen-minute delay, we began the wedding ceremony. I was sweating as I transformed myself from being a sheriff to a priest. As the long processional played and choreographed attendants welcomed a beaming, unknowing bride to the altar, I became a pastor. "Dearly beloved, we are gathered here to witness a most solemn and joyous Christian commitment. Let us pray for God's blessing." Later, the organist and trumpeter left following the wedding service with obvious disgust and a glaring look at me.

I've often wondered why I, a pastor, felt irrelevant in weddings. Pastors serve as event conductors and tolerant elders. I was relegated to performing a function with little attention to theology. The focus was on the wedding dress, the colors, the flowers, the pictures, and the reception—if dancing and alcohol were permitted. Yet, despite incredible wedding hysterics, some of my fondest memories are with the couple in pre-marital counseling sessions where the dynamics of marriage were explored.

The stories that pastors tell from wedding events are some of most hilarious and side-splitting in our lives. Don't get me started. From cats that were supposed to carry the rings on their tails, to a breastfeeding teenage bride who practiced the processional in her high heels, to bridesmaid's dresses that were pinned together instead of completely sown, to the wedding license packed and sent to California—the list of stories goes on and on. Most couples survive the wedding day and most pastors go home saying, "You wouldn't believe what just happened. I'd rather officiate ten funerals than one wedding."

Wedding Portraits

In my more than three decades of ordained ministry, I was a congregational pastor for about fifteen years and an administrative minister for the other fifteen years. In the congregational settings, officiating marriages was a regular duty. I required pre-marital counseling, usually four to six sessions, well before the wedding date.

For me, weddings were mostly theological dilemmas but also great opportunities for pastoral guidance. For example, what if one party was divorced and this was a second marriage? What if there was no visible Christian practice or belief by one of the partners? What if there were blended denominational memberships? What if there was a child or pregnancy already? What if another pastor would not officiate and I was the second choice? What if neither was associated with the congregation but loved the beautiful sanctuary?

In general, of the thirty or so weddings I have officiated, most of them had a "complicated" element to them.

Vignette #1

She was seventeen, about to be a pregnant high school senior. He was eighteen, a high school graduate about to go to college in a nearby state. Now what? Her Baptist pastor would not officiate the wedding, but her parents came to me and begged me to help the young couple. His parents, members of my Mennonite congregation, were in turmoil. "Please, please do something!" the distraught mother said.

In the end, I did lots of counseling. They had the baby and were married four months later in our church with me as the officiate. However, in the formal wedding portraits following the wedding service, the young bride held her baby but asked that I not be in the picture since "it's not natural to have a woman pastor."

Vignette #2

The couple was living together in campus housing. He was nominally Jewish and she was not churched, but they were very active in peace issues on campus. They came to our Mennonite congregation and asked me to officiate at their wedding following their graduate studies in May. The wedding would be very informal, in a park, and only their friends and some of their family would attend. "Just do the basics," was their request. However, they agreed to counseling sessions, which were joyous occasions as they explored their family systems and career decisions.

I pronounced them married on a sunny Saturday morning, even though they had inadvertently shipped the original marriage license to California in a moving box of belongings. I had to arrange a substitute license with the local judge at the last minute the Friday before the wedding. Oh, and their cat was held by the bride during the brief ceremony.

Vignette #3

She was Catholic; he a Mennonite. They planned a formal wedding at her very large church and invited both me and her priest to officiate. ("What would the Pope think?" I mused. This opportunity was beyond my ministerial dreams!) The detailed plans included choirs from both congregations, litanies and a homily by me, and a marriage covenant by the priest. It was a tremendously joyous event with both families collaborating on this unusual ecumenical wedding. The commitment to honor each other's faith values was evident. I stood beside the jubilant priest as he took my hand, held it in his while covering the couple's clasped hands, and said, "I now pronounce you husband and wife."

Vignette #4

A second marriage for both. Each couple had divorced, and our small congregation was shaken by those sad breakups. However, that sadness turned to joy when each found a new spouse and planned marriage. They were active in our congregation. Would I officiate? Yes, of course. I spent precious hours in counseling as a blended family with five young children (kindergarten through tenth grade) emerged.

It was to be a small wedding with little fanfare. The service was a simple worship service. The question of how to include the children yet be respectful of their tender feelings was solved with my suggestion that the groom walk in with his two children each carrying a flower of their choosing and placing it in a vase on the altar. Then the bride walked in with her three children also each carrying varying colors and types of flowers. They, too, put their flowers in the vase, which now formed a lovely spring bouquet centerpiece. The bouquet was not only a decoration, but it was also a symbol of individuals blended into one new family. I remember their wedding each spring with a deep sense of goodness after many hours of sobering reflection.

Vignette #5

I really liked the two single young adults who came full of energy, a sense of service, and a desire to be a strong Christian witness. He, a star college baseball player from a strong Mennonite family. She, a lovely, budding social worker and recent college graduate. Their relationship "clicked." The congregation was almost giddy with happiness as this "match" was overseen by onlookers and close associates. I suggested that we treat them to some form of wedding shower, and everyone prepared for a fun evening of warm wishes, good food, and storytelling. I proceeded to piece and then sew a log cabin comforter, which we gave to them at that church-sponsored wedding shower. This was the first quilt I had ever made. I felt deeply that this relationship was a beautiful blending of personality, faith, and values. Their wedding plans seemed perfect and good. However, many years later they divorced in a far-away city. That divorce still stings. I wonder what happened to the quilt.

Vignette #6

Two times, during pre-marital counseling, I "officiated" at engagement breakups. The first one was the member of the congregation, totally gifted and beautiful. Her fiancé was a local boy and her high school sweetheart. Now they were both in the community after graduating from high school, and they came to counseling faithfully. The wedding date was set and the invitations ready to be sent out. However, one day she appeared in my office. "Are you busy?" she asked as she stuck her bushy black hair in my office door. "Of course not," I lied. I gestured her in and closed the door. "What's up?" Tears stared flowing, and then she sat up straight, looked at me, and said, "I don't think I should get married."

I was startled but not surprised. I had identified quite a few areas of difference during our counseling sessions including faith commitments, financial goals, and desire for higher education. (She was graduating from college. He was not in college but was working locally.) I listened to her saga. She felt "destined" to marry her boyfriend by everyone in the community. They had been an item for years. But, as she grew older and expanded her horizons in college, she felt that her fiancé was not at all on the same life track she was on. "What do I do?" she pleaded. In the most careful tones, I suggested she tell her parents and that we tackle this very difficult topic in our next session. She agreed, and the couple came the following week.

I began the session in quiet tones. "She has something to share with you." With that briefest of introductions, she told him that she was not ready for marriage. He shook his head and said, "Well, then we shouldn't get married." I suggested that she take off the beautiful diamond ring and give it back to him. With that done, I took their hands in mine and prayed, *"Thank you, dear God, for love, for truth, and for courage. Bless Sam and Trudy as they dissolve this relationship. May you continue to be present in their lives as each goes on living separately. In the name of Jesus, I pray. Amen."*

The second broken engagement I "officiated" was rocky. She was a college student, and we had met in pre-marital counseling only once. He was a local boy full of bravado and a bit rude. His rough edges were covered with clever jokes and quips. She appeared mostly embarrassed by his juvenile behavior. Her conservative Mennonite background had been intrigued by a relationship that wasn't so restrictive, but as wedding plans progressed, her nervousness increased. I was uneasy, too.

Then one day, the church janitor said, "There's a young woman in the sanctuary and she's crying. I think you should go check it out." So I did. It was Sharon, weeping. I took her to my office, and, in tears and hiccups, she declared she was trapped and so unsure of a wedding to Dennis. "And he just smokes so much pot, and I don't like that." Finally, after an hour of conversation, silence, weeping, and tears, I suggested that the wedding was probably not a good idea. "You read my mind. I can't do this. I'll tell him tonight. You don't have to do anything. I can take care of this myself."

Sharon stopped by my office about a month later and thanked me for, in her words, saving her life. "If you wouldn't have been in your office that day, I think I would have gone nuts. I'm over it." She graduated from college, attended church from time to time, and fell in love. Now, years later, she is married and active in church leadership.

Vignette #7

One of my pastoral practices is to follow up with couples whose wedding's I officiated on their one-year anniversary. One fall, I organized a meeting of five couples and asked each to bring their wedding book of portraits to share with others. I baked a pan of brownies and had cold pop and water ready for the ten thirsty young adults. They greeted one another, and I led in some "get acquainted" conversation since some had drifted away from regular church attendance. They seemed delighted to meet with me. I also had notes from each couple's pre-marital counseling folders and asked questions like, "What's been the biggest adjustment?" "What did you learn about yourself in the past year?" "Was the wedding service what you expected?" and "What are your next five-year plans?" It was absolutely a hoot! They shared funny stories of wedding blunders, of food allergies, of financial decisions, and of conflicts about which apartment was really the best.

They opened and showed their wedding portraits. There was a squeal of laughter from me! There, in all five albums, was me smiling and wearing the same dress at every wedding. It was true. I had gone shopping for a dress that wasn't black or white or too colorful so I wouldn't clash with wedding décor. I ended up with a dress that was modest, had three-quarter sleeves, and was darker shades of purple and navy. I only wore that dress at weddings and, obviously, it had served me well.

The First Death

I was called to serve First Mennonite Church in Bluffton, Ohio, in mid-1994 and had nearly nine months to prepare for this new pastorate of a large congregation. The impending "birth" meant several anxieties kept recurring. One anxiety was the sheer impact of moving to a new community where I had no relatives and knew virtually no one. I had stepped onto the Bluffton College campus years earlier, but that hardly dented my memory. Who were these people? What were their names? What did it mean to enter the Swiss Mennonite immigrant congregation? How would this connect to the college? And on and on. . ..

Yet, one warning during the search process interviews kept creeping into my consciousness: "You'll do lots of funerals." The anxiety I had over this seemed out of control. I had very few funerals under my pastoral belt. I had only one. I had been in charge of an informal, non-traditional noon memorial service held in the city church fellowship hall for a neighborhood woman with few family members. I had no Mennonite congregation deaths in my nearly sixteen years of urban congregational attendance. These urban and university congregations experienced deaths at a distance—a parent, a grandparent, and my own father-in-law in far-away California just weeks before I moved to Ohio. I had also been assured by the receiving existing staff at the Ohio congregation that they would be at my side and assist wherever they could.

June 1, 1995, dawned. I was now the new senior pastor. Just five days earlier in late May, there had been a death in the congregation. So I attended as a guest to honor the congregation's loss and to learn as much as I could about funeral protocol. Now, to be clear, there is "A Way" to do a funeral in every congregation. Tradition, ritual, the local funeral director, and a host of familial expectations are wrapped up in funerals. Unlike weddings, which have much more consumer culture in them, funerals tend, still, to be locally oriented. My beginning June days stretched to July days and then to August and late into the fall. There were no deaths.

Some smart-mouthed friend said, "They're afraid to die with you around—it's just too interesting to have a woman senior pastor!" I pondered my own abilities in this new surrounding but secretly hoped no one knew my nervousness about funerals.

Then, on a cold, early January morning seven months later, the phone call came. A death. It had happened. This first time, it was a beloved elder woman whose family graciously said farewell in joyful thanksgiving.

Two weeks later, another death. This time, it was of an elderly man who had a heart attack while sitting on his living room sofa drinking his morning coffee. "He simply slumped over and was gone," said his widow as she told me her funeral thoughts.

The third death took only one more week. This time, it was the oldest member of the congregation who was living in a Toledo nursing home but would be coming "home" for the funeral and burial in the local cemetery. I had never met her, and there were precious few local family members left for this ninety-nine-year-old member.

Then one day later, a fourth call and another death. This time, it was of a local elderly woman who had a stroke. Would death ever stop its rapid course? Four funerals in January. Death became common and part of my pastoral identity. What I had feared became nearly normal yet so personal. It totally consumed me, and I survived and thrived. There would be four more funerals that year.

I learned from each funeral and gained the "Bluffton Way"—a worship service that honored God with thanksgiving for a life lived in our congregation's history. Each service was filled with scripture and hymns, usually "special music"—but not recorded music; a life story often told by a family member (from a script—not on-the-spot sharing); and a meditation and prayers by the presiding pastor—usually me. You see, the senior pastor seems to be necessary in death; an associate pastor will do only if the senior pastor is sick, hurt, or in India or Bolivia or Brazil. The family met with me (and sometimes other pastoral staff) to create a personal touch with favorite scriptures, songs, and tributes by appropriate colleagues, friends, or family.

The most unique and treasured tradition was the making of wooden caskets by congregational members. A "building" crew of (mostly) men made a simple oak casket using a diagram/blueprint created by a congregational member as a guide. The "lining" crew of (mostly) women carefully installed the fabric inside the casket with lovely folds in the lid and soft stuffing in the pillow and side walls.

The caskets were made in "builds" about twice a year so that a casket was always ready for a family without late hours of building during a time of need. One of my pastoral roles for the regular new member classes was to show them the "casket room" in the upper floor, which brought gasps and silence. However, the gesture of creating handmade caskets was a revered and intriguing option for this caring congregation stretching back to a previous pastor's leading. Simplicity and thoughtfulness combined to treat even the dead with love.

The local mortician was a Mennonite and easy to work with. He gave me great clues to the "First Mennonite Church Way" and coached my cemetery protocol. The tricky part was to control former professors who waxed on and on about their dearly departed colleague. Other marks: the service should not be longer than forty-five minutes; family should be seated in the center section but not ushered in procession—just gathered as for a regular Sunday worship service; the casket should be kept in the fellowship hall and not brought into the sanctuary, or, preferably, there'd be a burial prior to the memorial service; Saturday morning services would be immediately followed by a fellowship hall meal with a menu consisting of hot chicken casserole (if winter) or sandwich fixings (if summer), chips, salads (donated), and cakes (donated). The sharing of stories happened around tables after the meal with open-ended times of microphone passing that I, as pastor, led and closed with prayer. The trend toward cremation was strong, with handmade wooden boxes by congregational members most common.

I suppose they were fine, spiritual, and appropriate funeral events. I suppose I preached well and managed arrangements with the local mortician and congregational musicians. I suppose the bulletins had correct obituaries. I suppose I learned how to do funerals as worship. I think I became less anxious and more thankful for the congregation as the months passed by.

In fact, I learned to love funerals in a pastoral way. These tender times were taxing but immensely rewarding as families and friends, community and congregation, were bound together in a human bond beyond explanation. Old hurts, pains, and losses were sometimes healed with rituals of grace, joy, and even laughter. Memories were shared, stories were told, and pictures were displayed. Stillborn losses, old age, accidents, and disease merged into a congregational ritual of compassion, care, and mercy. No one was spared a dose of communal grace.

Every January, now decades later, I celebrate the call to minister at about one hundred deaths and memorial worship services.

Invisible

"I'm not really here. Please leave."

And with that, I was motioned out of the hospital room. I had made a pastoral visit to another church member, and as I walked down the hall, my eye caught a woman in a bed near an open hallway door. It looked just like Pauline. And it was.

I stepped into the room and greeted her with a usual line: "Didn't expect to see you today. I hope you are feeling better." The IV line was obviously sending blood from the hanging bag as she lay in the bed covered with hospital blankets. But instead of a receptive nod, I was summarily asked to leave. I left without another word.

I wondered what was going on. As pastor, I had not been notified of her hospitalization, and no family member had called to say that Pauline was in the local hospital. She was widowed and probably near eighty years old. Her brothers lived in town but attended another church. Maybe no one thought of notifying the pastor? Treatments? Cancer? Accident? I went back to the church office and asked the administrative assistant if there had been any calls concerning Pauline. "No, I don't think there's been anything." I dropped the topic and knew instinctively that privacy was an issue.

Several weeks later, I received a call from the funeral director. Pauline had died. And the next call was from her two brothers who wanted to meet with me to plan a funeral. "Of course. Please come to the church at 2:00 this afternoon and we will plan together. I'm so sorry for your loss. This is a surprise to me, too."

That afternoon funeral planning session was full of questions and shock. The two brothers and their wives had no idea that Pauline was ill. "What happened? Did she have a heart attack?" With caution, I shared that the death certificate, which the funeral director had shown me, listed "leukemia" as the cause of death.

"What? Leukemia? We had no idea! How long has she had this?" Many questions were asked with no easy or available answers. The family, however, noted, "Pauline was a very private person. This is just like her to hide things from us." We proceeded to plan a traditional funeral service, and they noted that her burial plot was beside her husband's, so at least that decision was clear.

The next day, one of the sisters-in-law called me. "Pastor, we went to her house to get the clothes for the funeral director's use. There, hanging in the closet, was a brand new, light-green dressy suit, lovely lace blouse, new shoes, and a note pinned to the sleeve of the jacket that simply said, 'funeral.' It's clear that Pauline had planned everything. We found her will and other financial records in two files lying on the large oak desk. Everything is clearly outlined and neatly arranged. She was so private but so caring."

Pauline desired to be invisible. Her passing, however, made visible her character, her strength, and her desire to assert her wishes—even in death.

Guns at Cemetery

Even though the surname numbers were unusually high in the congregation, they were mostly elderly and rarely in leadership positions. It was a strange-sounding Swiss name to my German-Russian ears, and I struggled to get the exact local pronunciation just right. My German language training needed to be stifled as I greeted them and quickly learned their first names!

I wondered about this large clan—several brothers, their wives, and then an assortment of next generation folks. They were reserved and quiet, often sitting under the balcony instead of in the main sanctuary. The women had their hair done at the same beauty parlor—with the tell-tale small curls and permanent frizz. Neat to a fault, their earrings matched the prim jackets, and the men always wore suits, white shirts, and ties. They did not clap for joyous children's stories, and they did not laugh out loud. They were very regular in worship attendance, and we could count on them to provide the necessary salads for funeral meals and to offer the words, "Good sermon," at the exit door as they shook my hand following Sunday worship.

One of the older men of that clan died late one Sunday evening at his home. I was called the next morning by the local funeral director with a quick report: "William is gone. Funeral here on Tuesday at 3:00 p.m." It appeared there was no discussion for this tall man and that his relatives didn't think it important to contact their pastor. So I called the widow.

She was solemn and soft-spoken. "Just didn't want to bother you," was her first confession. "We just want a simple service at the funeral home. Our family will attend, but we don't need the big church for this."

Pastors must read a lot into a few words. We have to judge whether there are really decisions that have been made or whether a momentary crisis has shielded thoughtful and traditional ideas. We have to wonder if there is a "church allergy," in that they really can't be in the church building for some reason or if modesty and low self-worth take over at death. The sub-text of humility is also one that says, "We really aren't worthy of church laments." We have to discern if this is about issues from the past—or present—or whether the funeral director, a highly-regarded local Mennonite, simply offered the funeral home for the funeral.

It's hard to say "no" to an offer of assistance. And so, ever so gently, I offered the congregational worship sanctuary and the fellowship hall for the usual lunch as gifts the church would gladly offer. I assured her of my services and my presence for the funeral. She said, "Please plan with the funeral director, and I'll see you at the funeral on Tuesday."

There would be no meeting for planning, no hints as to favorite hymns, no suggestions for life stories, and no offerings of connection to help this pastor. And, so, it all went smoothly, and we buried William in the local cemetery with mostly the large family standing quietly in the cold March afternoon.

Months later in the early fall, I received a call that another member of that extended family had a stroke and was in a neighboring hospital. I drove the fifteen miles and was ushered into the ICU section where Harold lay with multiple wires and obvious IVs covering his upper body. His wife hovered nearby and greeted me with worried eyes and an outstretched hand. "Thank you for coming. Harold had a stroke." I touched the visible arm and greeted Harold with soft words. "I'm Pastor Dorothy." He tried to open his eyes and moved his head in my direction. "Yes, Harold, it's Dorothy. No need to talk."

I stood close to the hospital bed, listening to the beeping, watching the numerous dials and gauges, trying to figure out the state of Harold's vitals. He was slipping in and out of consciousness.

His wife, standing on the other side of the bed, was tall and neatly coiffed but now had on a matching casual pants outfit—so unlike her Sunday attire. Her less formal clothes also led to less formal conversation. She motioned for me to walk to the waiting room, and I followed her as we found a corner for conversation. The description of Harold's condition was not good. The next hours would tell the tale of brain damage. The waiting had begun. We returned to the room where I offered a brief prayer for God's comfort and strength and for wisdom by medical staff. With the, "Amen," I bid Harold goodbye and assured Virginia that I would be a phone call away and would visit the next day.

The next week turned into a marathon of treatments, return of consciousness, and then a slipping away. My visits included one where Harold
responded to me with words and open eyes. Recovery seemed possible. But
then, one night, Harold stopped breathing and his earthly life ended.

The typical funeral planning was scheduled for the next day. Unlike
the previous funeral for William, this one would be following church tradition. As we gathered in the parlor for funeral planning, a group of relatives
accompanied the widow. Virginia brought nearly ten members of Harold's
family—a unique collection of some of our congregational members—but
most were relatives from other communities whom I did not know. Again,
my mind raced. Why all these people? What was really going to happen?
Were there family secrets that now would be shared?

After introductions and my usual litany of funeral planning decisions,
we proceeded with information. Yes, the service would be in the sanctuary.
Yes, there were some favorite hymns. Yes, the pastor could choose the scripture text for the meditation. Yes, the burial would be in the local cemetery.
But then Virginia opened up a large envelope and pulled out a form that
we ask congregational members to fill out. This helpful form gives dates,
schooling, and correct spelling of names and locations so important for the
printing of a memorial bulletin.

But Virginia noted Harold's handwriting on the line marked, "Comments." It said, "No guns at cemetery."

In a split second, I knew why the extended family was present. Virginia needed witnesses to hear her husband's wishes. And in the next
second, I recalled a visit to their home about a year earlier when Harold
had pneumonia and required hospitalization. I made a pastoral follow-up
call when he returned home but was homebound for a number of weeks.
At that visit, he chose to bring out the form from that same envelope and
noted the words "no guns at cemetery" to me.

He and Virginia proceeded to share their history that day. They had
been part of another Mennonite congregation in the community who ex-
communicated them when Harold joined the army in World War II. When
he returned from Europe, they (and the entire extended family of nearly
forty people) all joined the Mennonite Church where I now pastored. In
spite of its obvious pacifist teaching, my congregation had determined that
excommunication was not Christian and had allowed soldiers to join the
church—albeit with obvious different theological teaching and practice.
This, by now fifty years later, had created a church home for those who

marched in Veterans of Foreign War (VFW) parades and had fired weapons at an earlier war. As Harold leaned over and showed me the paper, he said, "My grandsons should never hear gunfire at my grave. I love them. They should never associate guns with me." And with that, he folded the paper and gave it to Virginia. The pronouncement had been made. The pastor had been dutifully informed.

Now, my mind reeled back to the parlor full of relatives; I repeated what Virginia had just read from the church form. "Is this what you want for Harold?" I asked. "Yes," she said. Then I knew I had to say something to the obviously shocked family members.

Before I could make a comment, a voice spoke clearly, "You can't do that. The VFW always has the gun salute at the cemetery." This strong stance came from a woman, much younger, and not anyone I knew. The next thirty minutes were filled with an intense discussion that ranged from hostility to quiet nodding and, finally, a direct question to the grieving widow. "Is this what you want, too?" And in a firm voice, Virginia said, "Yes. I honor my husband." And that was that. The dead and the living had spoken.

I don't remember anything about the service, but I vividly remember the cemetery. I noted the extra cars at the graveside, and I knew about six members of the VFW showed up. They respectfully stood by their cars with their military berets on, hands folded in a respective stance. I spoke the final blessing: "*Earth to earth, ashes to ashes, dust to dust, to earth you shall return, confident of the resurrection to eternal life through Jesus Christ. Amen.*" As folks stood to leave, the VFW brought the triangularly-folded American flag and handed it to Virginia. She shook their hands and acknowledged each one with a word of thanks.

She turned to me as all of the rest of the family members were entering cars and said, "Thank you. Harold wanted peace, not gunfire." I returned a blessing: "Peace be unto you."

Rural Pain

"Have you heard the news?" queried one of the woman preparing the picnic table. She and others were gathering for the traditional every-other-week congregational picnic in the city park.

"Nope. What's up?" I responded lightheartedly.

"This is no joke, but the news says that Rachel's brother was found dead this morning."

The picnic suddenly became a scene of lamentation. There was lots of hugging and tears. Expressions of shock, anger, dismay, and disbelief now rippled through the gathering crowd. Children seemed to sense something was wrong and were gently urged to go to the playground while the food was being assembled. They complied.

I was stunned. Could the reality of murder now be in Rachel's family? We had all been involved in the saga of Rachel's brother—a high school graduate who got involved in a right-wing militia group. I had listened to hours of Rachel describing the history of how strong-minded Midwest rural folks had begun to suspect government control and spying. This evolved into stockpiling weapons and arranging group meetings to learn about tactics of resistance and organizing protests. There were elements of Christian apocalyptic teaching and following God's rule.

Rachel's brother Thomas, an idealist who valued independence and self-sufficiency, had been lured into the group through friendship and a desire for belonging (according to my way of thinking). Thomas, and a fellow unemployed Mennonite, could not find jobs, a common problem among farmers in that region. Discouraged and broke, Thomas joined a group that was intent on challenging the system that seemed stacked against rural folks. In fact, this group used the Bible, and hence God's blessing, for their actions. So Thomas used his Christian upbringing and the teachings of Mennonites to align himself with this group. Rachel's family, specifically, was known to call out the government for over-zealous practices, targeting of racial minorities, and persecution of civil rights protesters. And so, young Thomas had carried out his own formation with absorption into a cult.

The tragedy leading to his death began when Thomas decided that the militia was on the wrong path and he attempted to leave the compound. The Order would not let him go, and the leader started an active campaign to keep him from leaving. This involved horrible rituals of beating, punishment, and animal cruelty.

Our internal focus shifted as someone spotted Rachel as she walked toward us. Our picnic circle was now opened as we absorbed Rachel with our hugs and tears. She choked out that Thomas had been found badly beaten, along with a child, age five, also dead. The horror deepened. "They killed them—both of them!" she stammered. "They are monsters."

We kept vigil with Rachel, and I finally asked the summer picnic family to join in a prayer for the meal (which we could hardly eat) and for Rachel. The prayer was one simple way to call on the Force of Love and to plead for comfort.

The Mennonite funeral held for Thomas later that week was large, and I sat in the "overflow" section of his home sanctuary as a guest mourner. I witnessed the stony faces of grief and the uncomfortable silence as the family's pastor tried to comfort a grieving community. Emotions were strong; relationships were strained; families united despite trauma. How could he join such a group? Why did he get involved in such a violent group? Why didn't he leave sooner? Where was God?

Rachel stood strong and stoic as person after person shook her hand and hugged her tear-stained face in the reception line of the meal following the funeral.

As the years passed, trial verdicts were delivered, and long jail sentences were imposed on the perpetrators. The fellow Mennonite who had joined the militia group with Thomas and then witnessed Thomas's death provided gruesome details. Why had he not intervened? Why didn't he stop the violence? Anger and hatred flowed freely among the survivor's families.

Now, after thirty-some years, I still hurt. This crime and these deaths happened to a family I respected and cared for. I recognized immediately that I could not journey deeply into the hell that Rachel was living in. However, I struggled mightily with the reality of pain, loss, and grief. I could learn of rural pain. I could stand with her. I could listen, care, offer conversation, and assure her that her God was suffering. The layers of hurt were like onion peels where a center was both protected but also bruised. Healing would take a lifetime. We remain friends to this day.

I also learned that deep pain sometimes means people leave a congregation—for a time, for a season, or, in some cases, forever. The seeming "niceness" of the congregation, the happiness, and the smiling faces, are just too much for those who are deeply wounded. They feel isolated, lonely, and rejected. Some feel shame, regret, and guilt. They cannot abide cheap grace or platitudes. God-language seems too casual and prayers seem trite. Moving to the edge of a community is absolutely necessary lest they disrespect their loved ones who are gone.

Pastors must navigate a journey of pain and loss with wisdom and patience. Most likely, pastors need to speak less and listen more. I learned to incorporate my congregation's pain into a repertoire of preaching, teaching, praying, singing, and leading. And never once did I blame the victim for their anger, fear, and hate.

I still pray for mercy for all the Rachels who wail all over the world.

Stillborn Dreams

I received a call from Step-mother Gloria, a term that connotes nothing of the extremely fond and loving parenting that Gloria provided for Christine and her brother Nathan, asking if I could come for coffee at their home that afternoon. "Yes, of course," I responded. I drove two miles to a lovely home on the outskirts of our village. Gloria and Phil, eager first-time grandparents, welcomed me, but I immediately sensed something was wrong.

I sat at their kitchen table with a coffee mug in my hand as soon-to-be Grandpa tearfully choked out the news that Christine's afternoon appointment at the obstetrician revealed no infant heartbeat. The child had mysteriously died in womb. Phil sat in the dining room chair, head in hands, repeating softly, "Not again. Not again." Fortunately, I knew that his own life was softened by the death of his first wife immediately after she gave birth to his son. I reached out my hand and gently caressed his shoulder. The sobs could not be stopped.

Christine was hospitalized and awaiting a birth. "Would you go and be with them at the hospital?" he finally pleaded. Of course, I would. After conversation and a prayer for strength and healing, I left them holding hands at the table, walked to my car, and drove to the hospital, a seemingly long fifteen miles away.

A stillborn death is most cruel. Months of waiting, of body changing, of hopes springing only to be dashed as life suddenly, often inexplicably, stops.

So it was for Dan and Christine. They were young, healthy, and vibrant. She, a local elementary school teacher; he, a musician-plumber with ready smiles and quick wit. Her own childhood had been bittersweet in that her mother died immediately after her brother Nathan's birth. Her father, then faced with a toddler daughter and a newborn son, remarried. Gloria, a college English teacher, and he, a college chemistry professor, raised those two siblings into confident, beautiful, and productive children. Christine, now in her twenties, had married her college sweetheart, and they both had shyly held hands during worship as they anticipated their first child. The entire congregation had joined them in joyful anticipation—now just a week away.

My mind was numb. What would I say? What would I do? What could I possibly offer to lessen this awful news? On autopilot, I simply maneuvered my car to the parking lot and walked into the hospital, directly to the birthing unit. A nurse motioned to the appropriate suite. There in the softly-lit room stood Dan, leaning into the bed where Christine lay with a swollen belly and with tears in her eyes. Her brother Nathan and his wife (whom I had married just two years earlier) were stoic at the foot of the bed, holding hands, silently sad.

It is times like this that a script doesn't appear. My Minister's Manual remained closed in my purse. I didn't even fumble for my Bible. All I could do was hug Christine and cry with her. So much sadness. So much loss.

Christine recovered first, shared her desire to give birth, and asked, "Would you come back when the baby is born? We'd like you to be present and pray with us then." Of course, I would come back. And after some conversation that highlighted the thankfulness for medical care, the health of Christine, the love of the family, and a desire to name the baby and then plan for a funeral, I left them to prepare for a birth.

I drove home, beginning the pastoral task of detachment. I needed to become steady despite the unfolding grief deep in my soul.

At about 2:00 a.m., my phone rang, and I slipped out of bed to another room where I heard that the baby was born. "Please come to hospital," said Dad Dan. "She is here."

Again, the drive in the dark night and on the nearly abandoned highway provided a womb-like atmosphere. So quiet. So deserted. So lifeless at that hour.

The emergency room doors parted. I indicated I was a pastor and there was an emergency in the obstetrics ward. More doors parted, and I was motioned to go right, then left and up the elevator. They sensed bad news and offered, "I'm so sorry for you," as I kept moving in the direction of stress.

I entered the room and found Christine in bed, holding the baby; Dad Dan leaning on the bed with his arm around Christine; and Granddad Phil, Grandma Gloria, Brother Nathan, and Sister-in-Law April surrounding the bed. I filled in the circle. It was dimly lit, and I could see tufts of dark hair as

Christine held a swaddled child. "We have named her Samantha Victoria," Mother Christine said in a hushed voice. "She was born about two hours ago, and we have had time to cry a lot and hold her a lot. She is beautiful in every way."

"The doctors say we will never know what happened. She is perfect," offered Dad Dan. In awkward, slow moments, conversation about Christine, the medical staff, and the experience of birth were relayed.

Finally, they asked for a blessing. I reached for the child as I would at any baby dedication, and they offered her to my waiting arms. I held the baby, peacefully sleeping in death. "*We praise you, O God, for we are fearfully and wonderfully made. We thank you for life, for family, for your love. We bless this child, Samantha Victoria, for she is precious in your sight. We ask your mercy in this time of grief and sadness. Be present to Christine and Dan, Phil and Gloria, Nathan and April. Surround them with tender care, and grant them strength and courage for these hours. We pray in the name of your Son, Jesus Christ, who lived, died, and was raised to new life. Amen.*"

I hugged the child and then, in blessing mode, passed her to Brother Nathan, who sobbed as he passed the baby to Wife April, who kissed the head of the child and passed her to Grandma Gloria, who lovingly passed her to Grandfather Phil, now weeping aloud as he handed the baby to Dad Dan, who held her in his big, muscular arms. "We love you," he said, and placed the child back into Mother Christine's waiting arms. The circles of life and death were intertwined.

We talked about a funeral and set a time for further conversation. Granddad Phil would build the small casket, continuing the congregation's tradition of making caskets at family's requests.

The congregation prayed for Christine and Dan the next Sunday as a red rose lay on the organ console—not upright in a vase as all births were typically announced.

The day of the funeral was a cold February morning, and a full congregation of mourners gathered for a worship service. A special version of "Jesus Loves Me" was played on the organ, which brought smiles and tears. I gathered strength as I stood, took a sip of water, and silently prayed that my voice would find life. I preached a meditation, and the congregation sang and spoke its faith and love. All of us had aching hearts. All of us were helplessly sad.

Following the service, we filed to the cemetery. As we unloaded cars and began walking to the burial plot, Dad Dan took the small wooden casket under his right arm and encircled Mother Christine's shoulders with his left arm as they slowly walked together. The tiny casket was lowered into the ground, and rose petals fluttered over the simple wooden box. "Ashes to ashes, dust to dust," I intoned. The infant dreams were now silenced.

Mary

Her quiet demeanor and nearly elegant posture were matched with a wardrobe that was fashionably smart and impressively designed. Often, she wore black, which, contrary to local custom, seemed New Yorkish and matched her dark hair. She regularly accented her dress with a single strand of pearls and used little makeup, but her deep brown eyes were warmly inviting. Being mother of four children—one in college (and married with baby daughter), one in high school, one in middle school, and one in elementary school—meant she was the primary caretaker. Mary was steady, focused, and respected for her teaching background and community presence. Her husband, David, was the town's physician—busy, well liked, and enormously popular.

The Saturday call from one of my parishioners came around supper time. "Have you been called about David?" she asked. I replied, "No. What's up?" And all she said was, "You better get to the hospital. David is in the emergency room."

I dropped my supper dishes and drove straight to the local town hospital ER parking lot and rushed into a crowded waiting room. High school students, members of David and Mary's Sunday school class, relatives, and friends already were milling around with eager but strained expressions on their faces. The four children were each being surrounded by friends and relatives. The oldest son was quiet. The oldest daughter, a high school sophomore, was crying and screaming, "No, no!" The middle school son was absolutely covered with his sweatshirt pulled over his head as he sat in a waiting room corner chair surrounded by pimply boys and squeamish girls. Little Marcie, a third grader, was being held by Mary's best friend, Judy. Something was terribly wrong.

My path cleared as I was ushered to the nurses' station. With a simple gesture, the charge nurse showed me to an ER treatment room, and I pushed the door into a scene of Mary standing near the gurney where

Dr. David lay motionless. He was not alive. She was alone in the room except for two nurses who now had streaks of tears running down their cheeks. They silently and professionally maneuvered things in the room, cleared medical equipment, and straightened the white blankets on their Dr. David. He seemed peacefully asleep. Mary stroked his forehead, ran her fingers through his curly dark hair, and called his name softly.

Her eyes met mine and I went to embrace her as she sobbed, her body shaking in tremors and waves of grief. "He didn't wake up from his nap," she finally said. "I was cooking, and he went upstairs to rest after raking leaves but didn't come down when I called him for dinner. I found him in bed asleep and tried everything, but it was too late."

In a matter of few minutes, Mary asked me if I would get children from the waiting room. Then she asked if I would please stay with her as her stunned children were brought into the sterile, cold room. Only the hysterical daughter made any noise, and they stayed away from the gurney until Mary said, "Come stand with me. Daddy died, and we couldn't do anything to help him."

The littlest one grabbed her mother's legs and buried her head, looking backward and away from the bed. The others simply hugged their mother and closed their eyes. It was impossible for the senses to absorb the reality. After many minutes, she deftly held her children, moved them to the door, and gestured for the two nurses to take them. Since they knew each other well, the children did not hesitate to respond to the nurses' gestures and open arms.

Mary and I and David were now the only ones in the ER treatment room. Struck dumb, we simply held each other and then, finally, she said, "I think I have to sign some papers." I volunteered to find out next steps and went outside.

The waiting room was now packed—standing room only. People were hugging each other, some softly crying. All eyes were on me as I exited the room. It became silent. "I'm sorry to share the news that Dr. David died from an apparent heart attack." Gasps and audible "no, no" responses erupted. The truth had been told. "Please stay as long as you wish. Someone please attend to the children. I will be with Mary, as she has decisions to make. Thank you for caring for the family during this very difficult time." I, now, was also on automatic trauma mode and tried to present a calm, reassuring, and professional tone. Death and life were mingled.

The nurse showed me to another conference room, and Mary was led in. She was shaking uncontrollably, so the nurse offered her a cup of water, sat her down in one chair, showed me the papers, left the room, and shut the door. Mary's eyes were already red, and tears kept flowing. I looked at the papers and saw they were about organ donation. "Do you want me to read the questions?" I offered. She nodded yes, but it was clear she was barely able to hear. Finally, I said, "There's a box here that simply says, 'donation of all useable organs, skin, eyes, etc.'" I choked as I read the sentence. Mary, quiet but grappling with her composure, said, "I don't know what to check, but David would want everything to be shared." I agreed and checked the "all" box, and she signed her name.

The nurse came back in and told Mary about next steps. The local mortician stepped into the room, greeted Mary with a hug, and said, "I am ready to care for David whenever you are ready." Mary simply nodded, and with a wave of her hand and a nod of head, said, "Please take care of David."

I sat quietly with Mary as the nurses came in and out with papers, instructions, and news that people were leaving the waiting room and the children were all with family and friends. Mary, already composed a bit, told me she would go into the waiting room and tell her children to go home. She would be driven home by one of her brothers—two of whom were standing in grief-stricken stances just outside the consultation door. Quietly, the crowd dispersed, the accompanied children left, and Mary said, "I'll talk with you tomorrow." She stood, took a deep breath, and went out with her brothers, one on each side holding her as they escorted her to a car.

I drove home, shaking as I turned into my driveway, just two miles from the ER. What now? Tomorrow was Sunday! What would we do? David and Mary were not only part of the congregation, but they were also part of thousands of people's lives in our region. The doctor was dead! How would people cope? And it was the Sunday before Thanksgiving with a full-throated plan for a harvest-themed worship service and offerings of thanks. How in the world would we be thankful?

Quickly, I contacted our minister of music, who already had heard the sad news. "What about our service?" I quizzed. "Should we change things?" After some conversation, we determined to begin the service with the obvious. I would share the tragic news at the beginning of the service. We would alter only a few things—change the hymn, add time of prayer, and temper the joyous celebration with a thoughtful service of praise for life, service, and community. I reworked my sermon late into the night.

After a nearly sleepless night, I awoke Sunday aware of the heaviness in my body. I looked at my notes for the opening to the service. Never have I been as glad as I was that day that worship was before Sunday school. We would gather as a whole community, children and all, to be one body as we started our grieving journey together.

After the choir entered the chancel area—fully decorated with cornucopia, wheat, corn, and orange and gold flowers—and the sanctuary was hushed, I surveyed the people, stood, took a drink of water from a cup hidden in the pulpit, and began. "Dear friends," I said and gestured with open arms as I stood behind the pulpit before a full, silent congregation. "This is a sad day. Many of you already know that Dr. David died last night of an apparent heart attack." There were gasps and other evidence that not all knew the reality of the dramatic death. "We are shocked and deeply saddened. There simply are no words at a time like this. There is the silence of mystery and the reminder of life's fragileness. We want to pray especially for Mary and the children today. We have lost our physician and we have lost a friend."

Then, in measured tone, I said, "Last Sunday morning, Dr. David was the physician who delivered infant Amber Louise, and that rosebud on the organ console this morning is in her honor. It is a fitting symbol of the beauty and the preciousness of life."

I breathed deeply, got control of my quivering voice, took another sip of water, and said, "Let us call on God, asking for strength and courage, for wisdom and compassion, as we journey together in grief. Let us recall God's many deeds of mercy, and let us be reminded that we are not alone in our time of struggle and grief. Let us bow in prayer."

"Almighty, Merciful, and Loving God: We are your people. We acknowledge your presence among us as we pray. We confess today that we are a confused and shocked people. We are overwhelmed with questions, and we wonder why one of your servants is now gone. We confess anger and hurt.

Great God, hear our prayers of confession as we also claim your love and grace. We accept in gratitude your promise—your covenant—that you will be our God. This day, we claim that promise because of the resurrection of the Lord, Jesus Christ. May your Holy Spirit work a miracle of comfort and strength to Mary and her children. Give them an extra measure of courage during these sad hours. Move in all our lives so that we will seek to be agents of helpfulness and friendship to the family and to others who call out for care.

Thank you for the visible body of Christ. Open our eyes to the poor and the hungry—especially as we can count such tremendous resources. Free us, as we plan and anticipate a new year, to love you more deeply and share your bounty more readily. We call on your name. Great God, hear our prayers. Amen."

Silence. I breathed deeply again.

"Our opening hymn for today has not changed," I gently announced. "'Now Thank We All our God' was written by Martin Rinckart (1586–1649) in 1636 during the violence and pestilence of the Thirty Years' War." (Wright, Lani, ed. *Hymnal Companion.* Elgin, IL: Brethren Press, 1996, 238.) "Rinckart, for a time the only pastor in the haven city of Eilenburg, sometimes conducted forty or fifty funerals a day. A fitting tribute, his hymn was sung after the Peace of Westphalia (1648), which ended the war. We sing this hymn as a tribute to a pastor from the past who knew sorrow and sadness. We sing because we are people of God. We sing today as a grieving people who are searching for hope. Please stand and sing together."

And so, the muted Thanksgiving service proceeded.

The following week was full of plans. A handmade wooden casket built by congregational members would be used. The visitation would be in our fellowship hall with their Sunday school class offering water and juice to guests. We would eventually welcome nearly six hundred people who waited in lines that stretched for a city block outside our church building. Mary's family, graciously, greeted everyone, although the children periodically escaped to the parlor or library to play, read, and be alone. Mary, noble in black with a single strand of pearls, stood near the open casket welcoming and receiving hugs, handshakes, and expressions of support. After hours of visitation, she went home to prepare for the funeral the next day. I was the last to the leave the church and went home to continue drafting the funeral meditation, with exhaustion threatening to overcome my best intentions.

Before the funeral service the next morning, we closed the casket. The children, one by one and assisted by their uncles, took the electric drill and drove the screws into the lid. Mary took her turn, then the brothers, and then others finished the process of securing the casket. It was done.

The sanctuary was overflowing. I escorted Mary, the children, and then the siblings and close relatives to the center front, which was flanked by hundreds of friends, all somber and strained. The organ music invited us to hymns of solace and generational strength. After the prelude ended and the ushers finished setting up extra rows of chairs in the overflow area,

I stood gripping the pulpit, weak-kneed, and gazed to the furthermost pew in the balcony. I needed to focus my eyes above the widow, now seated in the front row, hugging her youngest who sat on her lap.

I sipped my usual glass of water, took a breath, and read, "*Blessed are those who mourn, for they shall be comforted. God loved the world so much that he gave his only Son, that everyone who has faith in him may not die but have eternal life. There is nothing in death or life, in the world as it is or the world as it shall be, nothing in all creation that can separate us from the love of God in Christ Jesus.*"

The worship had begun; our tear-soaked journey had started, and I was standing with the people I loved and now needed to gently lead. "*God, be merciful,*" I silently prayed as the hymns were sung, tributes were delivered, and prayers were uttered. I, in a strange way, found my voice strong and my posture erect. We, together, would not let grief overwhelm us. As we took breaths together before each sung stanza, we were filled with hope. Voices sang with gusto by the last hymn. We were standing together as the family exited the sanctuary, now walking hand in hand but not weeping. I led the funeral procession to the waiting hearse, aware that I could walk and not faint.

The beautiful, crisp November day was a perfect setting for grief and thankfulness. Ohio's maples and elms were in full color. The cemetery was still lush green, but sporting leaves were crazily arranged among the tombstones. The walk from the hearse to the open grave was brisk as sunlight warmed our faces and tears. It was a brief committal service marked with the final act of lowering the casket while Mary and the children dropped rose petals and handfuls of black soil. The thud of the dirt remained the final sound of grief.

The doctor was gone; the hands of healing were cold and lifeless. The father was gone; the husband was no longer. Mary rose from her graveside chair, turned to me, and said, "Thank you. I could not have done this without you."

My heart melted as I embraced her. It was finished. Mary would survive. I went home and wept.

Four years later, Mary remarried. Ironically, his name was also Dave. I was on sabbatical and missed the intimate wedding where Mary and Dave celebrated their love after both losing spouses to death. The discipline of sabbatical separation was another kind of pastoral loss. The congregation was happy. The children loved their new father. Dave was handsome, vital, and caring. One young woman who longed to be married complained to me, "How come she gets two husbands, and I don't have one!" Ah, yes, the mysteries of life and love.

Then in just nine months, near Thanksgiving, Mary and Dave came to my office. Their faces were strained. He had been diagnosed with pancreatic cancer and given just months to live. Their love would be sorely tested, and the family would watch a steady decline as Dave lost weight, went through rounds of chemotherapy and then finally lay in their living room, dying, with hospice nurses in attendance.

The month of May dawned with spring blossoms, which he saw out of the bay window. He told me he loved spring and the smell of the flowers. He never complained; he endured pain. Mary, a constant presence in his room, delivered bits of food and cups of water and massaged his arms and legs with lotion. We prayed for comfort and strength. This death was slow and inevitable, predictable yet so tragic. I could not pray, wish, or hope away the reality that we all faced. The cruelty of disease could not be cured by the new local physician who advised his care.

Dave died in her arms on the ground floor just as her first David had died in her arms in the upstairs bedroom.

In another funeral procession, the children carried another wooden casket to be placed in the ground. Mary, standing straight and nearly motionless, threw rose petals on the casket as it was lowered into the ground. Her children gathered around her, forming a family hug.

I offered words of benediction full of grace and compassion. As I drove home, I struggled with the great sadness that kept me in tears. Mary, it seemed, was touched with the ironic blessing of two incredible spouses— but just for a short-married time. I remember her leaving the cemetery, dressed in black with a single strand of pearls. She remained steady, calm, and serene and faced death with faith and hope. What strength. What love. She was strong yet vulnerable, quiet yet visible, steady but struggling. In all of these phases, she expressed hope and love, compassion and caring. She did not shrink from public tears nor refuse gestures of friendship. While few words were spoken, she invited people to accompany her through her journey of love, then grief, then love, and then grief.

As a pastor, I, too, had to show strength when I felt very weak and lead when I felt traumatized and helpless. God's power was present, and I relied on both pastoral experience and the power of academic and professional training for just such times. Surely, I would be tested in my pastoral identity again and, ironically, I would gain new insights from those who grieve. Mary gave me strength.

Awkward

"Dad is fading. Can you come over?"

This began a several weeks' vigil for Raymond as he slowly died. His frail body wracked by emphysema meant horrible coughing spells. I guessed that he had smoked a lot as I entered the home for the first time. The scent of tobacco was unmistakable, and his daughter was embarrassed to admit that truth to me, their pastor.

He was a stubborn and proud man. "I really don't like that you see me like this," he uttered from his couch, all covered with blankets and crocheted afghans. "You don't have to come at all."

"I'm glad to come visit. Besides, you pay me those big bucks, so I better show up!"

He grinned and softened. "Okay, then. Come when you have time."

Daughter Ramona was the watchdog carrying on the roles of caretaker, financial manager, and medication dispenser. She was also the bridge for the rest of the family, who didn't attend church even though their names were on the membership roster. Ramona came by herself, often sitting under the balcony and about as far away from the pulpit as possible. However, she always shook my hand at the end of the worship service and thanked me. "Good talk or sermon or whatever you call it," she murmured and left quickly, seemingly uncomfortable with etiquette and church language.

This gesture of kindness was a bit startling since she had a gruff manner and a body that could handle the lawn mower, the chainsaw, and the ladders that stood against the garage. She was a painter during the spare time she had after clerking at the lumber yard.

As the days dragged on, I got a phone call. "Dad is dying. I can tell. Please come now." The two-story, white, wood-framed house obviously had been remodeled multiple times. I could see the odd rooflines. The windows on the front of the house were old and large, but the ones on the kitchen side were smaller and easy to open for ventilation. No air-conditioning was needed now. "Too expensive," she announced.

Inside, a dated collection of overstuffed chairs and brown paneled walls gave the impression of time stalled in the early 1970s. Newspapers and catalogues were piled on the coffee table near the couch—in easy reach of someone confined there. Various cups and glasses crowded the magazines. By the time I arrived, Raymond had died. Ramona was moving the furniture so I could stand near Raymond, breathless and silent.

Ramona's mother had died about three years ago, and her dad had continued driving to the country where he owned land and farmed corn and soybeans. He was a regular at the local bar where he ate his daily supper. "Sure glad I don't have to cook much," was Ramona's excuse. "It's great to share the house with dad, and that cuts my expenses." A mutual arrangement had developed, and the daughter had become a faithful caretaker.

"I called the funeral home. I didn't know what else to do," offered a helpless Ramona.

"You did just the right thing," I assured her. "Would you like for me to pray with you?"

A slight "yes" nod, and her sad eyes closed.

With that, I laid my hand on his unmoving chest and held Ramona's hand with the other. *"Grace and peace to your children who gather in this place. May you receive Raymond into your presence where there is no more suffering and no more hurting. Bless Ramona, and give her wisdom and strength in the coming hours and days. We commit ourselves to your Healing Spirit in this time of loss and grief. Grant grace to us. Amen."*

I no more had said, "Amen," when the doorbell rang. The hearse had arrived. In a matter of moments, Raymond would leave his house for the last time.

In the days that followed, a funeral was planned, and a worship service was held in the church. At the cemetery, I led the family to the open grave and waited until all the cars emptied. There was a large local family of cousins and a few close family members, most of whom were my parishioners, but I had never seen them in worship.

As I glanced around, I saw a woman nearly hidden behind a large tree about fifteen yards from the graveside. She was older with long braids, a western belt buckle, and an embroidered vest over a crisp white shirt. I walked over to her and welcomed her to join the gathering group. She nodded her head and said, "No, that wouldn't be proper. I've been his mistress for a while. But I couldn't leave Raymond—even now. I guess I won't serve him supper anymore." I acknowledged her intimate but bold excuse and retreated in stunned silence to a waiting family. I struggled to regain my composure and face the complicated grief encircling the open grave.

Death had its finality. Ritual had its place. I knew secrets had died that day, too.

We buried Raymond with a benediction as ancient as the bonds of love itself. *"Ashes to ashes, dust to dust, confident of the resurrection to eternal life through Jesus Christ our Lord. Amen."*

Another Beginning

August 1, 2015, I began an interim pastor position at my own congregation. It was intense, deeply satisfying, and yet troubling as well. I was jerked out of retirement and a more casual pace of life into an intense 24/7 routine. My new cell phone was now always with me; my datebook always in hand.

The first day on the interim assignment, a Saturday, I moved into "my" office—which included a new floor rug, a slight rearrangement of the furniture, and a quick tutorial on the computer. My cell phone rang.

"Hey, Dorothy," said another pastoral team member. "I'm sorry to bother you, but you're on call this weekend and I want you to know that Professor George is very ill and is probably close to death."

"Really? I wasn't aware he was so sick." After nearly thirteen years in administrative ministry with the regional area conference, I had not been close to death. I had visited a couple of pastors in the hospital as they recovered from surgery, but I had not been the attendant pastor to death itself. I gulped, put down my taco, and grabbed my car keys. "I'm on my way to their house. Thanks for the call."

It took only a few minutes to remember the demand of death—the labored breath, the ashen faces, the anxious family glances, and the awfulness of the clock ticking toward death from cancer. Yet, I quickened instinctively and grabbed my Bible. Which Psalm was right? As I drove, I rehearsed a short prayer for mercy for Professor George and said a prayer for "pastoral muscle memory" for me.

I was greeted by a friendly dog at the door as I was welcomed by the family, now already in vigil for several days. It was clear that we were bonded in the grief that gripped the family, but their resiliency and spiritual strength carried them. My heart was thankful for past associations and friendships with the family, a gracious gift from God, as I attended this first death in interim ministry. Words came easily, the slower pace of conversation felt comfortable, and I was swept back into being a congregational pastor like a summer Kansas breeze.

Day number two was Sunday. I preached and was welcomed with a litany cementing my new relationship with the congregation. I moved from pew to pulpit. Then, in the late afternoon as the sun was setting, the professor died.

While I knew that death and funerals were a significant part of our congregation's ministry, since our community was host to a large retirement and nursing facility, I was shocked how jolted I was by the starkness of death. The vigorous professor was seemingly smaller under a blanket. I barely recognized him as I was close to his bed during his last labored breathing and silenced voice. I was now emotionally drained and physically exhausted and, frankly, not prepared for death.

Yet, his funeral two weeks later was a huge pastoral joy. I moved through the worship with a sense of completeness and wholeness. The hymns—"For the Beauty of the Earth" and "In the Bulb There Is a Flower"—were deeply satisfying. The soaring of the clarinet with the chancel bells in wordless "On Eagle's Wings" was giving buoyancy to my soul. "For Everything There Is a Season" spoke the ancient prophet from scripture. The worship elements blended and were in tune with my own mortality, theology, and love of the congregation. I was "one" with the worship ritual, and the memory of being a pastor flooded back. This was what I was meant to be and to do.

During the next ten months, this pattern of death, funeral, and attending to the ministry of leadership during life passages, was repeated another twelve times. And each time, the shock of death, the ugliness of pain and suffering, and the blessed relief in death were followed by worship, pastoral care, and a spiritual renewal. I remembered, again and again, that pastoral presence was indeed a holy calling.

Of course, there was the usual routine of preaching, administration, and pastoral care for the interim assignment. I slipped into the role of pastor without much drama. I answered phone calls, drafted agendas, and kept a mileage log. I wrote endless reports, read committee minutes, and spent hours in consultation with other pastoral staff. The days flew by and the months melted into one another. Summer became fall; Advent became Lent. Then I knew that my interim assignment and calling were concluding by the next summer. I could not carry the role into another program year.

A new rhythm now occurred. I kept my cell phone off for days, and I didn't set my alarm clock. I started taking naps in the afternoons.

The release from the interim role included a gift from the congregation. It was a pastel print made by an artist in the congregation featuring a descending dove—"Pentecost" its title. Indeed, I had been hovered over by the Holy Spirit, and it was good.

June Deaths: The First Week
after Interim Pastorate

The month of June 2016 began with death—death of a pastor, a child, and then of a boxer. I knew two of them personally and the other one by reputation and influence. The impact of these three was astounding.

Pastor Steve died on the same day that my interim pastorate ended. It was a painful time in my life. I mourned the loss of leadership yet relished the lack of alarm clock wake-up calls. I mourned the things left undone at Bethel College Mennonite Church, and I celebrated the deepened relationships with congregational members. I hated the ending, yet I yearned for that ending for months.

This conflicted time matched my feelings of loss when I heard that Steve had died. Steve was a former pastor of my current congregation and a current pastor of my former congregation in Ohio! We were bound together as colleagues and lovers of the same congregations. Pastors die? A sixty-year-old dies? I remembered that Steve lived with a congenital heart disease and was quite ill for months—but death? It all was too soon, too sad, too close. My own mortality (facing seventy next year) seemed to creep into my mourning.

He was just about ten years old. He was a vibrant, energetic, and lively boy who filled a space with movement, quick actions, and ever-present wit. A car crash. An impact that was on his side of the car. Instant death. Instant quiet. The loss of a child's life is so hard to comprehend. Double the pain, as the mother was the driver. I was shaking with grief as I received a phone call from the child's aunt who was vacationing in Arizona and felt helpless at a distance. Did I know about the accident? Was a pastor attending the family? What could make things better? I hung up the phone and cried. I stood helpless—a pastor released from congregational service just eight hours earlier. My full desire was to run to the ER, to the church, to the family, and be present. But I was grounded in my home. I was banned from pastoral responsibilities. I was stuck with impossible emotions of release and of engagement. I could not turn off my pastoral heart. Later, I learned that our pastors were attentive; our church family responded with grace, care, and support. I could endure, although distraught.

Then, later that same week, Muhammad Ali died at age seventy-four, no doubt from complications of Parkinson's disease. This death, while very sad, was understandable and not surprising. This death, a combination of disease and organ failure, was normal, expected. However, Ali's life was larger than life! His influence as a boxer, a war resister, a world icon of Islam, was enormous and global. His death drew tears from those of us who never met him. I was impressed, again, to be reminded of his stand against the Vietnam War. He affected me. He strengthened my peace witness years ago—and now again.

The first week of June was marked with loss after loss after loss. I drifted from grief to anger to despondency to fatigue. I wearied of blow after blow of untimely deaths of three whose lives intermingled with mine. My professional pastoral life was concluding as well. This first week of "retirement" was surely an assault on my spirit. It was a time of transition—not smooth or gradual but sharp and immediate. It surely would test my resolve to be attentive to the Spirit's guidance.

CHAPTER 4

Rituals and Rhythms

"It seems like my baptism was more like a group shower than a personal bath. The experience held the seed of a committed Christian life. . . . At thirteen, I couldn't begin to understand this kind of personal commitment and discipleship. God knew this and didn't expect more than I could give. But whether we are thirteen, forty-three, sixty-three, or ninety-three, Jesus calls us out of the nameless chorus line into a face-to-face 'dance' with him."

Laurie Oswald Robinson in Duerksen, Carol, et.al. *Now It Springs Up—Spiritual Insights for Every Day.* Hillsboro, KS: WillowSpring Downs, 2007, p. 55.

Eating Bread

We were a small congregation in a midwestern university city. The oldest members—and were there just a few—were nearing retirement but still actively employed. The bulk of the seventy-five attendees were in their twenties and thirties, highly educated or working hard on degrees, and professional, so our family fit right in when I became the congregation's second full-time pastor. Our two daughters were entering third and seventh grade and each found a few peers in this church family.

The congregation was still on the "church plant" lists for three Mennonite-related area conferences, which, in itself, was nothing short of a miracle. The fact that a Mennonite congregation could claim support and allegiance to three branches of Anabaptism with three colleges—also located in Kansas—seemed a sign of God's delight and plan. We carried on trying to remain connected to larger Mennonite bodies yet also remain unique and distinct in our local witness.

Our congregation joined the summer church softball league and formed a "tri-affiliated" team, this time connected to the local Quakers and Unitarians to get enough players on our Mennonite team. We had purple t-shirts. Even I batted and fielded along with other decidedly amateurs, but it was fun—especially the snacks and the bloopers like missed pop flies. And, we won the championship one summer! Go Pacifists!

We worshipped in a campus ministry building where we shared office space with the Lutherans and the United Methodists. We maneuvered chairs and furniture as different groups used the large gathering space. Each Sunday, my car trunk was filled with posters, bulletin boards, bulletins, handouts, and altar decorations that were then unloaded, used, and then reloaded to go back to their storage spots. After storing all the folding chairs following worship, our family exited for a local restaurant lunch. Go Movers and Shakers!

We established rituals of welcome since I had determined early on that I was "planting" a church each fall as new students, graduate assistants, and professors joined the university community. One such ritual was the creating of a table the first Sunday in September—our "Welcome" Sunday. The floor at the front of the huge rings of semi-circle chairs was covered with pieces of two-by-fours, cut in varying lengths. The modest wooden music stand was center-left. My sermon was based on the gathering and sending of disciples, probably from Luke 10. And then the ritual of communion began.

On cue, several people came forward—a deacon, a student, a child, a professor, a charter member—and stood behind the wood pile. As I read a litany of welcome, each person began picking up a piece of lumber. Together, they notched a table—a simple, plain wooded table that resembled saw horses with a table top. The pianist took a folded, red and white checkered cloth from the top of the piano and unfolded it onto the table. A picnic-like atmosphere, joyous and pleasant, emerged. A baker who was a member brought a loaf of bread and a pitcher of grape juice and set them in the center of the now ready table. Ah, we were going to celebrate the Eucharist.

Who would be eating bread? The children, already leaning forward or whispering into their parents' ears with a desire to eat bread, watched with eagerness. Guests, first-time students, were cautious. Were they welcome at the table? Charter members and core leaders were ready to be served. And so it was. I pronounced the invitation:

"You are welcome to this table. This is not our church's table. This is not a table for insiders or those who have been here before. This is not a Mennonite table but a table for Christians from all backgrounds. This is not a magic table with fancy bread or wine. This is the Lord's Table. This is the welcome table. All are welcome here. You don't have to be a member here. You must, however, claim to be a follower of Jesus Christ, and by eating bread and drinking juice, you are declaring that you will be transformed and changed to be more faithful in your Christian walk. Come, take bread, dip it into the chalice of juice, and eat with joy."

Most all came forward in a slow, steady line, but some of our young children, including mine, did not—because they had not been baptized. This reflected a profound teaching from Anabaptist roots that believers declared their willingness to die for their faith as they joined with Christ in communion. No child can make that pledge, and so they waited until baptism—believer's baptism.

The service ended with a rousing hymn and a benediction of peace to all. People began dispersing in lively conversation and casual greetings.

Ironically, however, eating bread did not end. Somehow the Lord's Table had become the Children's Table. The children, now a cluster of nearly ten youngsters, were gobbling up the bread and laughing as they pulled apart the last of the large loaf where adults had picked out minute pieces to taste. They each had nearly a handful, and one even shared it with a two-year-old who smiled broadly as she waddled away with bread held high. The absolute joy and spirit of being a church family came through loud and clear. No adult stopped them from eating bread but rather stood at a distance and smiled. I wiped a tear from my eye. My children were enjoying Eucharist.

In the end, the loaf disappeared, and everyone left—filled.

. . . and the Greatest of These
Is Banana Bread

The teenagers sat in a circle around the small table in the center. I held up a loaf of bread and said, "This is the body of Christ."

"Whoa," said one smart-aleck sixteen-year-old boy. "That looks like banana bread to me!" The rest of the students in the membership class learning about Mennonite theology and practice were now all giggling and smirking. Ah, the pastor had been found out!

"Yup," I said. "Banana bread it is. We are going to talk about communion today. Remember last week we talked about baptism, what it means, how we do baptism—and some of you did not like the idea of being immersed—and how, in this congregation, you can choose the method or mode of baptism? Well, today we going to talk about what it means to participate in communion and why we do this ritual in the church."

I broke the loaf in half. "Why did I do that?"

After a quiet moment, one girl offered, "I think it means that the body of Jesus was broken for us."

"Right. Now I'm going to hand one part of this to you, and you can pull a piece from it and eat it. Tell me what that means."

Slowly, the group received my outstretched bread and ate silently. "What did you think about when you were eating?"

Just as slowly came some thoughtful replies. "I am trying to be like Jesus—not being self-centered."

Another pondered and then offered, "I don't know if I'm ready to take communion. I don't think I can be like Jesus."

(Oh, how I love teaching! Oh, how I love these kids!)

"Okay," I continued. This time I'm going to put the partial loaf on the tray, and I am going to ask you to hold it and offer it to the person next to you with these words: "Take and eat, remembering Jesus."

So very quietly, so very slowly, the tray went around the circle of eight. One girl (Isn't it always a girl?) teared up and couldn't say the words. She looked at me and said, "Sorry, I don't know why I'm so emotional. I guess this communion stuff is about really deep things."

(Oh, God, how fearfully and wonderfully we are made.)

I then pointed to the goblet in the center of the table. I also had a tray of tiny glass cups filled with grape juice. And, just as with the bread, I repeated questions.

"What difference does it make if we drink from the same cup?" And, of course, Mr. Smart-Aleck had to say, "We'll all die from hoof and mouth disease!" Chuckle. Chuckle. "And what difference does it make if we all drink from our individual cups at the same time?"

It was a catechism experience of deep meaning and experiential learning. As we left the room, the sassy-mouthed one asked, "Do you think it would be all right if I took the bread and told my parents about today?"

"You bet. Take the banana bread. It's kinda special."

(Oh, God, how thankful I am to be transformed by the Bread of Life.)

. . . and a Little Water
from the Jordan River

The traveler brought the water to her sister. "When you decide to be baptized, this water could be used." A sister in the flesh was becoming a sister in the faith.

But the younger sister struggled with the questions of faith (not unlike most teenagers). How does Christianity stack up against other religions? Where is God in all of this? How can I witness when I am unsure of the answers? Am I ready to be baptized? As the pastor who taught, I was humbled by the profound questions. The struggle was intense. The questions were real. The answers were complex.

This year, it seemed the students were more philosophical. They were deeply interested in the questions of "truth," of "salvation," of "doctrine." They asked about the nature of God, about the Bible's stories, about hypocrites in the church. Where would faith be demonstrated? Could baptism occur when the questions were so deep and the answers so unsatisfying?

On Maundy Thursday, with prepared statements and trembling knees, five of our youth stood before the gathered body of Christ. With bread and grape juice aromas mingling with spring rain air, the room was rich with atmosphere. One by one, they spoke of their faith and their assurance that Jesus was with them. Some recited a favorite Bible story (Joseph reconciled with his brothers), others remembered church life (camps, service trips, Sunday school, worship), and others felt that something was right about their relationship with Jesus Christ ("I wasn't ready last year; today I want to tell you that I am ready to be baptized into Christ's body.").

The five distributed bread and juice to the quiet tables of eight. We broke the bread and shared the cup. We were becoming a new family.

It was after the communion service that she came to me with a shy grin. "Dorothy, you might think this is kind of silly. My sister brought some water back from the Jordan River. She was on a study tour with Bluffton

College last November, and she said it was for me to use when I got baptized—if I wanted it. I'm thinking that I would like to use it on Easter Sunday—if that's okay with you."

Barely able to listen to her plea without jumping up and down with an enthusiastic "yes," I waited until she finished her request.

"Absolutely—yes!"

On Easter, they knelt. The deacon held the clay bowl fashioned by the father of another who knelt. As the water dripped off their heads, five young people experienced a little local water mixed with some from the Jordan River.

The local bowl and the global water became our link with each other, the world, and the Christian memory of Jesus' baptism.

"In the name of God, the Creator, Jesus the Redeemer, and the Holy Spirit, our Sustainer, I baptize you with water. Amen."

Vulnerable Preaching

"I want to say that this sermon is exactly why our church is not growing. It was depressing and certainly not inspiring. If you keep preaching like this, our family will leave." With that, the father of three young children and husband of one of our deacons sat down. I was standing at the wooden music stand that served as a pulpit in front of the semi-circle of seventy-five worshippers. I gripped the stand's corners and said something like, "Reuben, thank you for your sharing. We have lots to think about."

It was the season of Lent, and I had decided to preach a six-week series based on Richard J. Foster's book, "Celebration of Discipline: The Path to Spiritual Growth." I chose from the dozen options in his provocative list of inward disciplines (meditation, prayer, fasting, study), outward disciplines (simplicity, solitude, submission, service), and corporate disciplines (confession, worship, guidance, celebration). The Sunday on simplicity turned out to be a mini-disaster.

On top of that, the custom in our small congregation of university-related folks was the opportunity to respond to the sermon after a moment or two of silence. Generally, the comments were casual: "I really appreciated the sermon," to thoughtful: "I need to study that text more," to critical: "I really disagree with your conclusion and would like to talk with you about it."

In other words, five minutes of sermon response was not only expected but generally respectful and presented in the spirit of Christian discipleship. This custom was not something I instituted but inherited from the previous pastor. The worship service was meant to be participatory and inclusive and reflected the academic bent of the attendees. He had every right and expectation to express his opinion about my sermon.

However, that Lent service proved to be so uncomfortable because I knew why he was so angry with me. I could not share with anyone his wife had appeared at my front door weeping late one afternoon earlier that week. I invited her onto the front porch, so our children would not witness the conversation.

"He's having an affair with one of his employees," she blurted out. "It's happened again."

I could not comprehend what she was sharing but held her as she wept. "What happened? Are you sure?"

"Yes, I'm sure. I saw them together at a restaurant after he left a note saying he couldn't come home for dinner because of work. I noticed the pattern of late-night work over the past months, so I drove around and saw his car in the parking lot of the Holiday Inn."

She went on, choking out words, and then got angry. "I hate him for what he does to our family. We probably will be moving away since that's the way he solves the problem. He confesses and promises to be faithful. He finds a new job, we move, and we start over."

I promised to support her, and she quickly dried her eyes and said, "Thank you for being here. I love the church, but I'm sure we will be leaving. You are a great preacher." With that, she left the porch and drove away.

Then, the Lent sermon on the spiritual discipline of simplicity proved to be anything but simple. The shock of his public preaching accusation was evident to all. In a small congregation, attendance patterns and "growth" are not merely statistics; they are constant struggles and strains. Conference subsidies demand attendance numbers. Supervising church planters suggest strategies to grow a congregation and to expand programming. There are yearly visits from external funding sources, which are anxiety-producing. I, as a female pastor, was sometimes the cause of people leaving the congregation or not even attending in the first place! Theological differences about gender, biblical interpretation, and social witness were all factors that made a difference in who attended and who left. So, when a father stands and announces an intention to leave the congregation, the whole congregation is hurt—loss of a family, loss of income, loss of children, loss of leadership.

Preaching is a community event. It is still the revered part of most Mennonite congregation worship experiences. Pastors undergo tremendous pressure to preach prophetically—but not too personally! The biblical text is supposed to become fresh and insightful—but not be too intellectual. Sermons should be thorough but never more than twenty minutes long.

Yet, I love the rhythm of preaching—the preparation, the digging into the Bible text, the application, the actual composition. I love the intrigue of ancient words and ancient settings that challenge contemporary listeners. I love the worship service creation with appropriate hymns, prayers, and rituals. I love presenting the Word through sermon. But the minute the sermon is over, I inwardly fall apart. I want to disappear. I want to retreat. I am so vulnerable that my stomach aches, which is why I eat oatmeal every Sunday morning, and my mouth is incredibly dry. Week after week, year after year, I stay engaged in the whole order of service. I end the service with the traditional greeting of the parishioners and endure the comments at an exit, which I can hardly absorb because I am overwhelmed with vulnerability.

In the end, that family moved away because Reuben got a new job in Pennsylvania. I encouraged the social committee to plan a farewell reception for the family. I met with Reuben's wife several times as she coped with the trauma of adultery and then relocation of the family. Our unsuspecting congregation promised to send them to their new community with our best wishes for safety and new friends. I prayed a new congregation would welcome them. I held in my heart the pain of the family and continued to preach as the Spirit led. Not one other person in the congregation ever scolded me for a sermon. But, sometimes, preaching results in loss.

I remain a vulnerable preacher.

Thanksgiving Mess

It was a balmy November day as I drove a red Ford Fiesta down the interstate to a Mennonite church. I was to be the guest preacher for their annual Thanksgiving Festival, which included a worship service, a noon potluck with an area sister Mennonite congregation, and then a "church growth" seminar that I was to lead in the afternoon. I had flown to this western state and rented a car at the airport for this excursion. In the back seat of the car was a large bookbag filled with a sermon, a Bible, overhead projector slides, handouts, and several relevant books. I had the radio turned to a local station that played traditional Christian music.

A car passed me, and I glanced at my speedometer, which was indicating sixty-five miles per hour—the speed limit. "They must be in a hurry to get to church," I mused. "I wonder if they are coming to listen to me preach!" But just as quickly, a highway patrol car passed me with lights flashing. With a firm signal to me, the officer pointed to the side of the road. He passed the car in front of me, and that car, too, pulled to the side of the road.

I was nervous. What had happened? Had I missed a lower speed sign? I grew panicky. I was in a strange car in a state far away from home, alone. Traveling to speaking engagements in new places, or to urban hospitals to visit suffering parishioners, has always given me huge anxiety. I tape the exact directions written in large black marker to the dashboard so that I can find the location with just a glance. No way to consult a map—and this was long before I had GPS and a soothing voice to guide my driving. I have no mechanical skills, so a car breaking down or even a flat tire would nearly paralyze me with fear. I hated late-night meetings in a city where gas stations required credit cards and pin numbers before buttons and levers could be pushed and pulled. Simply standing outside of a car in a strange town, city, or airport was nerve-wracking. I'm also a stickler about being on time. Efficiency and time management go out the window when others take control of my driving times and cause delays—such as a train slowly moving through the town causing traffic to halt or road repairs that mean waiting for traffic to move.

Of course, this Sunday, I worried about being late to the church service. I did not know any of these people; I had never visited this place; I had no knowledge of the current issues facing the congregation. Yet, I could guess that a rural congregation might be struggling with attendance, the economy, or leadership demands. I fumbled for my driver's license as the officer stopped at the driver's window of the car in front of me. Before he looked at any of their documents, he walked to my car and I rolled down my window.

"How fast do you think you were going?" he quizzed me.

"I think about sixty-five. There's no cruise control on this rental, but I'm pretty sure of the speed."

"Well, madam, you were going sixty-seven. I clocked you. We have speed laws in this state, and you should obey them. I'm just going to give you a verbal warning this time, but let's try to be more careful in the future."

And with that, he motioned me to drive away as he started pulling out his notebook and walked to the car parked in front of me. I sat there shaking a bit. My heart was beating fast, and I reached for my water bottle. With renewed focus, I gently steered my car to the highway and cautiously drove in a nearly deserted stretch of interstate. I would be on time at the church—but just barely. Welcome to Sunday stress!

As I stopped in the church's parking lot, I noted my sweaty hands and blouse. I was greeted at the main entrance by an usher, and I said, "You are a little friendlier than your highway patrol officer," I quipped.

He just laughed. "We should have warned you. That patrol officer catches folks on Sunday morning, and we know there is a speed trap set. All of us have been stopped at one time or another. Sorry for your inconvenience, but that makes you one of us!"

"At least I don't have a fine—so I can still give my offering this morning," I joked halfheartedly.

I tried to gather my bulging bookbag and my jangling nerves as I entered a building. Finding the bathroom for a required calming moment helped me gather my belongings and my guts. Loneliness and vulnerability were causing indigestion, and I found Tums in my purse. With a deep breath and a short prayer for strength, I walked to the waiting pastor for instructions.

I was given a bulletin and told to follow the pastor's cues. "You'll sit with me on the stage—and please do the pastoral prayer as indicated in the bulletin." That request was news to me, but, of course, I could pray as well as preach!

As I sat in front surrounded by cornucopias, straw bales, sunflowers, and baskets of fall flowers, I felt as if I was on a parade float being viewed by the congregation. I surveyed the congregation as they began to file in. The wooden pews could hold at least 150 people, but, I guessed, no more than fifty people were worshipping that morning. They, as if allergic to each other, were spread out so every pew had empty spaces. From time to time during the service, I could see women standing in the back of the church with aprons on. They stood for a while and then, after looking at their wristwatches, slipped back down the stairs to the basement where smells of onion and sausage already filled the sanctuary. Clearly the meal had priority over worship that day.

I preached to the attentive few, but, as I tried to remain focused, I noted two women on the right side of the third pew from the front. One was obviously silently crying as she blew her nose and dabbed her eyes. The other woman had her arm around the weeper, and they sat squished together.

Now, as a preacher, I have endured lots of distractions while preaching. Once, a mother changed the dirty diaper of her infant quite deftly on a table at the rear of the church. Another time, a man fainted, and ushers carried him out to a waiting ambulance. Coughing, sneezing, babies yelping, coins rolling on the floor, cell phones ringing, hearing aids squeaking, whispering, hymnbooks dropping—well, it's a noisy sanctuary sometimes. However, this weeping pair was hard to ignore. I finished my sermon and regained my front stage seat.

The pastor thanked me and then led the service in a time of sharing prayer concerns. After the usual litany of hospitalizations and medical problems (which preachers often call the "organ recital"), the two women moved to the pulpit. I was sure there had been a death in the family—or some dramatic illness.

I was busy taking notes, as I would be the "pray-er" after all the informal sharing. (While it's the business of pastors to pray, even unceasingly, it's inhospitable to have a guest preacher perform prompted prayer in a place where intimacy is expected and relationships are critical to spiritual nurture. I love to pray publicly, but the drama of impromptu prayer is often, at its best, hollow and forced. The Holy Spirit still, however, does its work.)

What happened next is difficult to recall. The weeping woman read a letter that was an accusation of sexual abuse she suffered by a deacon of the church. I was stunned as she pointed to the man/deacon (a stranger to me) who was sitting in the third row on the left. She was now sobbing. The comforter-woman, who stood with her, finally completed reading the letter as the survivor could not continue speaking. They left the stage and resumed their position on the right side of the church. The elderly and portly deacon, with a white shirt, black suspenders, and a dark tie, did not move or react. His white hair and folded hands seemed frozen in place.

The pastor nudged me. He whispered, "This is the time for you to pray."

The rest of the service and my prayer are lost to me—deeply buried in a sacred spot where I hold pastoral moments of chaos.

The potluck gathering in the basement was quiet and awkward as the neighboring congregation arrived with casseroles, cakes, and salads. The stunned hosting congregation could not hold their shock, and I witnessed the guests trying to guess what had happened with anxious glances to me.

I was again asked to pray to bless the meal.

Sensing the perplexing moment, I decided to delay my required prayer with a word of explanation for the emotional state of affairs. I explained, briefly, that there had been sharing in worship that included a shocking accusation of sexual abuse. I assured everyone that I would meet with the pastor (I guessed that I would do that later in the afternoon!) and we would offer care, comfort, and a thorough investigation. Meanwhile, we would welcome each other to this joint meal with Christian brothers and sisters and then meet for a seminar after the meal.

I must have prayed mightily—but I could not swallow any potluck food. More Tums were needed.

The Thanksgiving mess of a traffic stop, guest preaching, abuse accusation, seminar leadership, and then processing with the pastor, was beyond comprehension or movie script.

As I drove my rental car back to the airport city, I wondered how in God's name the church would survive and whether I really was equipped to live out my calling to pastor. Exhaustion was my traveling companion, but I kept my eye on the speedometer.

Three Ironies of Advent

The guitarist had quietly strummed the final strains of "Silent Night, Holy Night" to a hushed congregation and prepared to exit the stage when a hearty wail from a baby pierced the air. The choir members tried not to smile as the wails escalated into full-throated, choking screams from an infant in the back of the sanctuary. How could this infant know that there were too few "silent" nights? How could this congregation miss the obvious irony of a melodious, ethereal musical score and the equally high-pitched cry in quick succession? I was humbled by the unplanned response to a perfectly beautiful song. Beauty and anguish—the themes of redemption.

Then, looking around, I saw several hundred people preparing for worship, mostly dressed in black. Prompted by our pastors to symbolize "Black Lives Matter" in our worship experience, many displayed black attire. However, those without email and our morning guests were clearly in the minority, dressed in sparkly sweaters, red blouses, and winter plaids. One woman, thoroughly embarrassed by her non-black outfit, wondered how it could be that everyone else got the message, but she did not. The realities of those "wired" were obvious; she was not in the email system of the church. Our desire to stand for justice had also created an ironic injustice.

The children's choir sang a wonderful rendition of "Let There Be Peace on Earth," but what caught my eye was the girl wearing a black shirt with "Dream" printed on it in glittery turquoise letters. In the middle of the song, I focused on that word while her attention was fully focused on the director—oblivious to her strong witness. Did this child lead in song and word? Did she know her church attire was also a public declaration? After all the adult words, prayers, songs, and proclamations, maybe a child will lead us to peace on earth.

Guest Preacher Hospitality

"Here we go," my roommate Sharon noted as she put her guest key into the hotel room door lock. The door opened to a very modest room with one desk, one chair, and a double bed. "I guess we'll be sharing everything!" This was the first meeting of a major inter-Mennonite committee. It was the policy of most Mennonite agencies to share rooms and even beds to save money.

The hotel itself was near the interstate and the Chicago airport, so noise was constant. With traffic congestion and airplane takeoffs and landings, we knew our two nights would have many interruptions. I was delighted to get to know Sharon, a competent executive in the denomination. However, sharing "everything" made me anxious. Was she a talker? Or a snorer? What kind of routines did she have? How would we manage showers and alarm clocks? I knew, from many previous committee meetings, that these "little" things could make for stressful accommodations.

After that first meeting and our first two nights together, we looked at each other as we packed our bags for the airport. She said it first: "Not again. I have too many reports to prepare and phone calls to make. It's not possible to be quiet since I am secretary for this committee. No more sharing rooms."

And I chimed in, "Not again. I sleep so lightly that any noise is disturbing, and I was responsible to chair the meetings. I need my sleep and some downtime. I really am glad we got put together, so we can clear the air. I agree. No more sharing rooms for me."

After that, I always requested a private room for any overnight meetings. The denomination sent me a bill for the extra room, which I paid gladly. Those "donations" gave me peace of mind, privacy, and the ability to lead meetings knowing I was better prepared and less stressed. I even learned to pack a nightlight and small noise machine. Frugality was not the highest value—self-care was.

Being a guest preacher in congregations was also an opportunity for experiencing hospitality. As a conference minister, I traveled a lot. Since our area conference included thousands of miles in geography, many Saturday overnight stays were required to be ready for Sunday worship—and Sunday school presentations, search committee orientations, and Church Board special meetings. Weekends were scheduled full.

One time, the host family lived in a lovely ranch home in the country. Spouse Richard had accompanied me; he frequently drove while I rehearsed a sermon or made notes for meetings.

"Here's your room. Sorry it's so crowded, but we store our Christmas tree in here, and I have a collection of dolls and teddy bears. Aren't they cute?"

We gazed in the small guest bedroom and saw that there was simply a one-person path into and out of the room. Obviously, with floor-to-ceiling shelves of knick-knacks and large dated furniture, the room was for storing seasonal décor. The walls were covered with framed photographs of their children's sports awards, school class projects, and ancestors from long ago. There were people all over the walls!

Our suitcase would be put on the bed until we got into the bed and put the suitcase back on the floor. It was a bit disconcerting to see many doll eyes and teddy bear button eyes staring at us as we invaded their space! We maneuvered ourselves into the room, and that evening we planned our sleeping pattern. I would leap over the suitcase and crawl to the side of the bed firmly against the wall, and then Richard would lower the suitcase and climb over it into the bed. We giggled as we wondered how we would reverse motions in the middle of the night or early morning. We slept soundly amidst a silent, attentive audience.

Another time, I had flown to another congregation to preach and then meet with the search committee, as their pastor had resigned. I was hosted by a family with three children—all in later elementary school and junior high. The very modest home did not have a spare bedroom, but instead they had fashioned a sheet to hang over the arch to the living room. I would sleep on the hide-a-bed in the living room. Unfortunately, their two cats roamed all night, and I was awakened more than once by a curious cat on my legs or pillow! In the morning, their single bathroom was shared by all six of us. The order of baths and timing in the bathroom was scheduled, and I, last in line, followed the junior high boy.

"Your turn," he shouted through the sheet.

"Okay, thanks," I answered and paused from rehearsing my sermon.

And with that, I inherited the bathroom. He left all his clothes and underwear on the floor; the bathtub had clearly not been cleaned, as dirt and soap rings were evident and the wet towels were hung over other towels. The sink was full of toothpaste, and I gagged as I tried to brush my teeth. Showering was a cleansing act.

It was clear to me that the children had not been told how to clean or care for their own belongings and, more importantly, how to care for a guest. I was gracious and thankful for a safe place to sleep, but between the cats and the bathroom, I was glad to leave their home.

My favorite overnight accommodations were those hosts who simply said, "Here's a room for you. Your bathroom is here. You do not have to talk with us because we know you have preparations. We have a congregational potluck tomorrow, and that will give us plenty of time to chat. There is juice in the refrigerator and snacks for the evening. Breakfast will be ready at 8:00 a.m., and we will get you to the church at least thirty minutes before the service starts. Have a good evening." With that, they left me alone.

True hospitality like that honored me as I dealt with stressful situations, complex relationships, and often new worship patterns and pastoral expectations. They were strangers to me, yet I dearly loved meeting the variety of people in our area conference. It was a joy to learn about their congregations, their histories, and their dreams for the church. A good night of rest made everything a bit more manageable.

I have often reflected on the visit Jesus had with Mary and Martha (Luke 10). Hospitality included feeding people and hosting guests (Martha) but also listening to Jesus thoughtfully (Mary). Both attended to their guest(s); both provided the best of their talents. Being good hosts means more than a bed and dinner. It means paying attention to the basic physical needs while honoring the leadership gifts of the guest.

Still Praying

It all started innocently. We were on staff retreat. Eight of us were sitting in an un-air-conditioned conference center sharing our goals for the next year. This day was a good one: lots of sharing; lots of reflecting and re-membering; lots of dreaming—and even a little scheming! But the question I had posed was this: "How can we make the Vision: Healing and Hope statement* come alive at our congregation this next year?"

> *God calls us to be followers of Jesus Christ and, by the power of the Holy Spirit, to grow as communities of grace, joy, and peace, so that God's healing and hope flow through us to the world." (Mennonite Church USA Vision Statement, 1995)

We focused on the goal to "enrich our prayer, worship, and study of the scriptures." I suggested encouraging people to read the Lectionary scripture texts for that week (always in the previous Sunday's bulletin). And, I sug-gested, we would begin our regular Tuesday morning staff meetings with a devotional based on the next Sunday's scripture texts.

That led to a suggestion that maybe some people would like to join our devotional time—or at least be aware that the staff was focusing its spiritual energy at that time on certain texts and that we were praying for each other and for the congregation.

"But people work. They have children to get ready for school. No one can be here at 8:00 a.m."

So, I casually suggested, "Then, let's meet at 7:00 a.m.!" The general hoots and laughter subsided. They knew their pastor well. I hate—well, dis-like—early rising.

One thing led to another. We decided to have all four Lectionary texts read, and then follow each reading with generous amounts of silence. The "morning prayers" would begin at 7:00 and end promptly at 7:30 a.m. I would bring orange juice, Elaine would make coffee, and we'd have Paula (who was beginning a baking business) furnish cinnamon rolls. Everyone would gather in the sanctuary for readings, prayers, silence, and reflection, and then we would gather in the fellowship hall for fresh rolls and coffee.

The first Tuesday, September 2, 1997, there were twenty or so people there—plus the staff. We had a wonderful experience praying together, listening to the scriptures, and laughing over "early" morning coffee.

"It was the first week," I said at staff meeting. "Next week there will be only a few. And, finally, when it's only staff attending, I will declare that this was a nice idea and we're back to 8:00 a.m. staff meetings. No more early mornings for me!"

January 1999. We are still praying at 7:00 a.m. We have never had less than that original number of twenty, and generally there are nearer to forty pray-ers. The only Tuesdays we have missed were the first weeks of January this year when the blizzards shut everything—including schools, college, businesses, and highways.

College students, some with wet hair and droopy eyes, are there. One parent in a family comes one week—the other parent the next, alternating child care and prayer time. Some are "older" folks who drive in the darkness of winter from Pandora—seven miles away. Some are farmers who are used to the early morning hours. An attorney, sometimes in formal business suit, prays. A jogger, on her way for a country run, stops for prayer before continuing her exercise. Music—organ, piano, solo voice, flute, congregational singing—has been used. A candle is often burning. The sanctuary lights are purposely dimmed. It is quiet. There is no commentary. We always pray the "Lord's Prayer." We always stand to receive a benediction and blessing as we leave the place of praying.

This regular prayer ritual has become a valued part of our ministry in the congregation. Even those who cannot attend (or will not get up that early) sense that focused prayer is happening. We receive requests for specific petitions and offer intercessions in that early morning hour.

I know that prayer has always been offered in our community. Now I know it even happens at 7:00 in the morning.

(According to the First Mennonite Church, Bluffton, OH, website, Tuesday morning prayers at 7:00 a.m. are ongoing in 2017—twenty years later.)

The Congregation in the Airport

Gathering

I was able to survey three rows of passengers awaiting our short flight from Chicago to Fort Wayne. With plenty of time on my hands, I decided, after reading someone else's newspaper, simply to watch people.

To my left, a family of three spoke in quiet Spanish to each other, checking their watches repeatedly. Soon, an airline attendant wheeled another passenger, an elderly woman, to the single vacant seat beside the husband of the family. She took her place in the row of four. They greeted each other politely and fell silent. Finally, the conversation began, and I overheard the introductory words. He said the reason for the family's trip was a wedding. His anxiety was growing because the flight's delay meant they might miss the wedding altogether.

Praising

The friendly grandmother remarked that weddings were important times. The husband said, "Families are the most important thing."

Grandmother quickly added, "Well, next to Jesus Christ, of course."

Husband smiled and turned to Grandmother saying, "I agree." In heavily-accented English, he noted that they were Catholics and Jesus Christ certainly was the reason for families.

(*"Hey, I'm a pastor,"* I thought. *"Would you like to discuss religion? Your faith? I have lots of experience with these matters." But I remained silent.*)

Grandmother hesitated, and then mused, "Your people are Christians? I thought you said you were Catholics."

Proclaiming

Husband replied, "You got that right. That's why we're going to this wedding. We need to stand by our young people. We need to tell them that if they don't have faith and if they don't begin by being married in the church, well, they aren't getting in touch with the real power for their lives. We dropped everything just to go to this wedding."

Just then, the announcer declared another delay. The family threw up their hands, but smiled at each other, and Husband said, "Well, we'll still get there for the reception! But we're going!"

Praying

Meanwhile, a middle-aged woman, dressed in a business suit, stepped to the ticket counter, asking, "Another delay? When will we leave?" She was assured that the flight would leave within thirty minutes. She promptly turned to the row to my right and sat down. Her cell phone came out of her purse and she started dialing. I watched as she simultaneously reached for a handful of tissues, dabbing her eyes. Her call was not answered. The tears continued, silently forming. Woman took off her glasses, wiped her face, and sighed deeply.

Next to Woman was another couple, loaded with packages from their cruise. Complete with a straw hat, posters, and shirts full of flowers, they were the picture of returning vacationers. "I can't believe it. We traveled for three weeks, connected with planes, buses, ships, and never missed a connection. Now we have one last hour to fly, and we are delayed for the third time," Cruise Husband declared to Weeping Woman.

Weeping Woman could not hide. She said, "And I just have to get to Fort Wayne. My father just had a heart attack. He's in the hospital, and. . ." her voice trailed off. The glasses were once more removed, and the tissues covered her eyes.

(*"Hey, I'm a pastor,"* I thought. *"I've dealt with emergencies, death, and such. I'll help." But I remained silent.*)

A business man, with attaché case and computer bag, was sitting in the middle row, with his back to Weeping Woman. He turned to Cruise Couple and Weeping Woman and shared, "I've flown this route a hundred times. This is Saturday night and we're low priority. Just hope the plane even flies!"

A collective groan from Hispanic Family, Grandmother, Cruise Couple, and Weeping Woman filled our small waiting area. We all exchanged knowing glances, checked our watches, and fell silent.

Again, Weeping Woman took out her cell phone and could not make connections. And again, we noticed her sorrow. Without bidding, she said, "I have to get to the hospital. I just have to." Her voice was soft, pleading, and full of pain. "If I can't reach anybody, I'll just take a cab and get to the hospital as fast as I can. I'm sure everyone is already at the hospital anyway. At least I hope someone is there."

Offering

Business Man again turned around and said, "Ma'am, I'm from Fort Wayne, and it might be tough to get a cab in quick fashion. I'm driving right by the hospital on my way home, and I'd be glad to drop you off. It's really not out of my way."

Weeping Woman, somewhat dazed, replied, "Thanks, but I'm sure my family will get me. . .maybe," and fell silent.

Later, after two more delays, we boarded our flight. It turned out that I was seated next to Business Man, Grandmother and Hispanic Husband were next to each other, and Weeping Woman and Cruise Couple were in the same row. Our little "congregation" was together among sixty other passengers, almost in the same seating pattern as in the airport lounge.

Witnessing

We fell silent, drinking our sodas and chewing our pretzels. As the plane finally landed and prepared for departure, we stood together in the aisle waiting for the doors to open. Business Man turned to Weeping Woman four rows away and again said, "I'll be off the plane before you. I will go to the parking lot, get my car, and pull up to the curb. If you want a ride, meet me at the baggage claim curb. It's really not out of my way. I'd be happy to give you a ride."

Weeping Woman, looking very tired, weakly smiled at the stranger. "Thank you. You are very kind."

Sending

I managed a quiet "Amen," which Business Man acknowledged with a slight smile.

(*Hey, I'm a pastor. At least I could give the benediction.*)

She Died Without Me

Pastors often talk about "surviving" Advent and Christmas seasons. They are quick to take vacations or at least take a couple of necessary days off in the new year. However, my new year was beginning not with vacation but with a four-month sabbatical from pastoring.

January 2, 2000, was a wonderful day of closure and preparation. I sat in the congregation that Sunday, free from responsibilities. Just before sharing in Communion as a ritual of first things in the first of the year, I was called to the front. The Staff Relations Committee chairperson was also there beside me. He explained, again, that this marked a transition time for the congregation, the staff, and for me. I was invited to share my sabbatical plans in broad outline. Then, together, we participated in a litany of commissioning for the sabbatical time. I was released from pastoral duties. I was encouraged to rest, to study, to travel. The congregation empowered the staff and repeated the interim plans for leadership. We prayed for God's wisdom, guidance, and protection for this time.

I returned to my pew and received the bread and the cup. It was a time of filling up and of letting go. It was good.

How Could She Die Without Me?

Monday morning began with sleeping in. This luxury was not unusual since Monday is my usual day off. But this time, the waking up was even more gradual, more deliberate, more delightful. I relished this unhurried time. Exercising felt good, showering was refreshing, and dressing seemed unhurried.

So, it was the next day when the sabbatical began. I slept in again, missing my usual Tuesday 5:30 a.m. wake-up call. Casually, I sat down to toast and hot coffee. I began to read the morning newspaper. I scanned the headlines and went to Section B. And there, in the obituary column, was the announcement of the death of a long-time member of my congregation. I gasped, put my coffee down, and stared at the page. How could this be? How could she die without me?

The telephone had not rung on Monday. No doubt, she had been actively dying. Even though she suffered from Parkinson's and had languished from time to time, she had not been in crisis during December when I was very available. The newspaper column seemed larger than life. And the telephone never rang.

Struggling to Disconnect

I struggled all that day (and week) with disconnecting from a congregation I loved. Now the starkness of death presented an overwhelming temptation to do something, to fix something, to be present somewhere, to reconnect. I paced. I sat down. I stood up. I paced some more. I reached for the telephone, but I resisted that temptation. I prayed for strength for the family and comfort to those who mourned a loss. It was the first lesson of a sabbatical for this pastor.

Pastors on sabbatical, staying in their small hometown, must develop a new routine, a new pattern, a new identity. Was I a pastor in hiding? Was I still a caring person? What would the family think and expect of me? Certainly, I had full confidence in the pastoral staff and congregational members. They knew exactly how to care for a grieving family. Everybody would take their parts seriously and respectfully. Plus, the congregation had included, in its initial memorandum of understanding, the provision for a sabbatical leave as part of its pastoral personnel policy. This was not their test. It was mine.

Acknowledging the Need to Let Go

Over the course of the last five years, I had developed a pastoral identity appropriate to a large congregation (membership of six hundred) in a college town. The pastoral staff and program staff are competent, visionary, and hardworking. We enjoy a high level of collegiality. A sabbatical, thought I, maybe was not really necessary. If we have such a good thing going, why mess it up with a four-month sabbatical? Why try to fix something that wasn't broken?

On the other hand, the five years had been exceedingly full ones. The congregation had increased its average worship attendance by more than 20 percent. We had increased our program staff by combining two part-time program positions into a full-time associate pastor staff role. We were doing strategic planning and putting into place the next five-year vision.

Alongside these congregational demands, I had personally served at the denominational level in a key leadership role. That responsibility had demanded about twenty to thirty days of travel per year. I had to admit that, although invigorated and gratified by these significant ministries at both the local and denominational level, I was tired. Maybe a "leaving behind" of those years would take a structured rest, and even two or three weeks of vacation would not be adequate. Maybe a "letting go" of that energy, that commitment, and commending it into God's hands was the work of my sabbatical.

Pastoral identity can get all wrapped up in "doing" while neglecting the "being." Even though I have religiously taken my Mondays off, slipped into my sunroom for an occasional mid-week afternoon nap, and enjoyed movies as escapes from my job, the unrelenting pace of pastoring takes its toll. The interruptions at all hours of the day or night with emergencies, often resulting in death, were frequent. I had officiated at more than forty funerals—burying dear friends, stillborn babies, and the suffering elderly. It was time, especially for me, to take a sabbatical.

Having just become more comfortable with my professional identity as a female senior pastor of a large congregation, I had to step back and reassess, maybe readjust this role. The nurturing part of me felt guilty for leaving "my" people, even if just for four months. The liturgical part of me hated to give up worship planning for Lent and Easter. The social part of me truly missed the conversation, lunches, and yes, even the committee meetings. Sabbatical represented some losses to my identity.

Opening to a New Pastoral Identity

My first week of sabbatical left me floundering for a new identity. This death gave me a quick lesson in self-definition. It also gave our small town (population 4,500), including the local funeral director, and my congregation an immediate opportunity for adjustment. Plus, the interim congregational leadership plan had to be implemented without delay.

I relaxed into a pastoral presence from a distance that first week, entrusting the work of the church to others with deep confidence. I faced a less busy time with openness. I lived with an emerging "pastor on sabbatical" identity.

God's strength and blessing had accompanied my now-departed friend—and me—for many years. Our relationship had grown from being strangers to becoming friends in the faith. She died without me, but she died well. I faced my own pastoral identity for this sabbatical time and found a new, emerging one. I was also living well.

(Reprinted by permission from *Congregations: The Alban Journal,* July/ August 2000, published by the Alban Institute, Inc.—www.alban.org—)

Confirmation

The sabbatical (May-April 2000) was a time to step back and, in a sense, take a new look at myself and my vocation. I have not doubted my pastoral vocation in my current assignment. Yes, there are days of discouragement, of tension, and there are even hours of deep fear. How can I be a pastor when I have many faith questions? How can I preach when the biblical text is complex and the contemporary applications murky? Why should I be a leader when others are smarter, more faithful, and less anxious? Will someone find out that I have doubts? But, overall, I have thrived in this vocation and sensed that God is leading and guiding—even if I can only see that in hindsight.

An identity that is so focused on public roles can begin to take over any kind of self-reflection. I knew that my time in Bluffton was not over. I was not using the sabbatical time to "look for a better job." I knew that this was just the right calling for this time. I knew that my spouse was happy in his vocation—a wonderful sign, since he "followed" me for the third time. Our children, while far away, were seeking their own life callings and seemed contented in their places. Even extended family, farther away, were healthy and enjoying retirements (parents), careers (siblings), and growing up (niece and nephew). So, there was nothing that beckoned me anywhere else.

The current lead pastor role at First Mennonite Church is one that has evolved over the five years. I worked with fifteen different staff people—adjusting to resignations, finding interim staff, searching for new staff, and finally orienting new long-term staff. Things seemed "new" all the time and hardly routine. I seem to thrive in the change, and so I knew that a major dramatic change for me was not imminent.

However, confirmation, a sense of re-commitment, was my yearning. Could I find in this sabbatical a confirmation for my current pastorate?

Could I understand and yield once again to God's call to my present vocational placement?

The confirmation came in unexpected ways.

I attended a continuing education event for senior pastors of large congregations conducted by the Alban Institute. Known for its careful research, writing, and workshopping, I was prepared to learn new things. I flew to San Diego in late January for a week of rubbing shoulders with other senior pastors. Forty-eight people (including eight women) gathered in a historic mission church setting and promptly dove into theory and practice.

Confirmation came when I was already anticipating the teacher's next comments. Confirmation came when suggestions were made for how large congregations should be pastored and I discovered we were already doing most of the suggestions. Confirmation came when I raised my hand to answer, "Yes, my congregation has a sabbatical policy—and I am on sabbatical right now!" I found my experience to be a minority one. Only a handful of pastors there had such a policy, and even fewer had taken a sabbatical.

A second confirmation came in South America. I was attending a Mennonite congregation's worship service in Recife, Brazil, one Sunday night in late March. I listened to the Portuguese singing, praying, and preaching—understanding almost nothing. I could sense their spiritual joy and commitment, but I could not communicate. As the hour went on, I noticed the banner hanging in the center of the front wall. I tried making sense of it and realized it was advertising for a Bible lecture series. A text was in quotation marks, which I surmised was a key Bible verse. "Jn. 8:32" was easy enough to figure out, so I turned in my Bible to that text. And there it was: ". . .the truth will set you free." I knew that verse! That is the motto for the college in my congregation's town! Sitting in Recife, Brazil, I read the motto for Bluffton, Ohio. Connection and confirmation.

A third confirmation was my incredible yearning to go back to work each week. I missed my job. I missed familiar worship and the people. I was ready to reembrace the congregation. The deliberate waiting for May 1 became a gradual gearing up for beginning again. I felt less stressed and more rested. While I dreamily thought of being independently wealthy and living in a log cabin somewhere in the woods, I also knew that leaving congregational life would be only loss for me now.

Allergic to Church

For once in my life as a pastor, I simply walked out the door and stayed put in the same community where the church is located. After a ten-month interim pastoral assignment, I took a three-month "sabbatical." Our denomination suggests an absence by pastors who retire or leave their congregations after a term of service, and the implementation is nearly uniformly embraced. On the pastor's final Sunday of service, there often is a formal "covenant-breaking" with a litany of release and blessing. Pastors do not appear in the congregation for the next days, months, or even years; they do not conduct weddings or carry any visible leadership roles. The "new" pastor takes the waiting mantle of leadership from day one.

In all my former pastoral leavings, I also physically moved to a new community. With our previous "sending" congregation's assistance, including heaving boxes of books and belongings onto a moving van, I often left my beloved community and drove away. In some cases, we drove nearly a thousand miles. We made a clean break.

I recall one pleading phone call about two months after arriving in Kansas from a young man whose wedding was planned for the next summer back in Ohio. "Would you please officiate at my wedding? You baptized me! You were a great pastor to me. I really don't know the new pastor. I want you!"

My heart was breaking, and I said, "I'll think about it, but I'm not sure I can make it work." I hung up. I had lied. In no way was I going to return to officiate a wedding. It was part of my "covenant-breaking." I would not participate in the life of the congregation even for a friend's son. I called him back the next day and said I was not able to be the pastor—and we shared a final, loving goodbye. My heart was breaking, and tears flowed as I realized how deep my bonds were and how badly those bonds could succumb to pressure.

That summer, however, I stayed put. We did not move. I announced that I would return to my congregation as a "pew person" on September 1. The summer was mine, and the pastoral ministry office was not mine. However, I was not relinquishing my membership in that congregation—I was giving up the role of lead pastor, a temporary shepherd office. After all, we had at least four former pastors sitting in the pews each Sunday. Our congregation had a good track record of re-entry after months (sometimes years) of absence. Pastors knew their boundaries, and the congregation loved them back into the fold without demands or expectations. I thought I could do the same.

What developed in the next weeks was a visceral allergy to church. I became nauseous just thinking of entering the building of my congregation. I had absolute dread when I thought of going back to church. We had planned travel to Minnesota and to Colorado the first weeks of June, so the temptation to even drive toward the building was not an option. I loved being hundreds of miles away. I experienced periodic bouts of weeping and nightmares of wandering in the sanctuary where no one appeared for services. I avoided emails and bulletins. I had a mental block to anything "church," and wished I could move away and live like a hermit in a desert somewhere. Well, actually, I wanted to move to an apartment in the city with many conveniences, and I fantasized about a Kansas City condo. Maybe I should move! Maybe I should volunteer at some food kitchen where no one knew me but where I would have a job, a purpose, a station. I was wildly imaginative about escapes. I feared staying local.

On several Sundays later in the summer, we drove away. Once, we ate a delicious, bountiful breakfast at a renovated fire station in a nearby city. We were among other folks, enjoying huge pancakes, buttered home fries, and crispy bacon. Food satisfied my soul, and the strangers all around us seemed comforting and welcoming. The efficient waitresses moved through the crowded tables and booths with arms ladened with massive servings of biscuits and gravy or mounds of scrambled eggs and slabs of thick ham. It was a feast. Ordinary folks, some who arrived on motorcycles and others in family vans, all seemed right at home on the cement floor with an old fireman's pole within eyesight. One waitress guessed we were first-timers, so she shared a little history of the building and then poured another round of dark coffee. "You come again!" she chirped as we left our cash and a generous tip.

It all seemed like church. The "sanctuary" was ready for anyone who opened the door. The "communion food" was served by "ministers," and the bill became the "offering" of the morning. I could get used to this kind of congregation.

Another Sunday morning, we drove seventy miles north and remarked how lush, green, and beautiful the Flints Hills were. It was summer, but this year the rains were plentiful and the crops healthy. Wheat fields now were harvested, unlike in May when the golden sheaves waved in the Kansas wind. I, of course, rarely saw a Sunday countryside, and the sheer magnitude of the hills brought me strength and thanksgiving.

We drove past the country cemetery where I had conducted my last funeral in May. It seemed oddly important, as it provided a marking of a now silent community. On the hilltop, with cars and trucks zooming by, it was a symbol of permanency and peoplehood. Ruth was there, safely held in the soil of the prairie. Her husband, beside her, rested after years of service to immigrants, Spanish speakers, and budding churches in South America and Texas. I knew they were surrounded by other Mennonite believers who now formed a quiet marker of history on the Plains.

However, I still could not and would not step into my congregation's hallways. I promised to abstain from presence, but my promise now seemed a promise to leave. I was conflicted about my role, my past service, and my capacities to preach or teach or heal or pray or administer. I felt sick about my allergy to church and wondered if giving over pastoral leadership was also giving away my ordination.

In our Mennonite theology, pastors are part of the congregation. They are in the community as they lead the community. The simple practice of the pastors actually sitting in the pew and then coming forward to preach, often without pulpit or stage, reflects the integral binding of pastor to the people. We spend inordinate amounts of time locating pastoral leadership in a search process, emphasizing "fit" and "match." This marriage metaphor marks language and practice befitting courtship and "falling in love." The installation services for new pastors talk of a new "covenant." We're not kidding. Once in, you're in.

But from my earlier pastoral exit experiences, this leaving was quite problematic. Previously, I was "called" to a new congregation in another state. I was "called" to become a seminary administrator. I was "called" to become a conference minister, a "bishop" in most religious language. But each of these calls meant a leaving, a goodbye, and a covenant-breaking.

I experienced divorce. Congregational members pleaded, "Why can't you stay?" "What did we do to you?" "I promise I'll say 'yes' next time to serving on Church Council." "Don't you like us? Don't you love us anymore?" "Do you think you'll ever find another congregation as good as we are?" The match now seemed inadequate. Those I left behind felt betrayed. And I was leaving with guilt and doubt, too.

However, this summer, I didn't pack boxes or drive away. This summer, I slept in my own bed and opened my mailbox each day. I did not move. In fact, I was stuck. I yearned for hours of silence and slept most afternoons away in long naps. I was physically, mentally, and spiritually exhausted. I could not have moved very far even if I had wanted to.

My allergy to church yielded to September by sheer will and determination. I walked into the sanctuary on September 4 and confidently sat down. The hymnbook in my hands was oddly reassuring. The chancel bells softened my heart and reminded me of music's ability to soothe and comfort. The Labor Day focus on the integration of worship and work was a great "welcome back" homily. I needed to integrate my life again. The warm handshakes of those around me welcomed me.

I didn't sneeze and I didn't cry. My allergy was gradually subsiding. However, I knew I had a limited time to be present before I would want to escape to a waiting car. It would take time to create a new covenant.

CHAPTER 5

Surprises

"At this time (1969), the Mennonite denominations as a whole were not able to be of much help to me with questions of faith and sexuality. Mostly there was silence on the topic. Raising the question openly, particularly among Mennonites, was somewhat like questioning heaven and hell with my mother at the dinner table. However, once again I was drawn into space hospitable to honest questions, space first within other-than-Mennonite theological communities, and later within the Mennonite church itself. In time, I found ways to stand with integrity and love as a Mennonite Christian woman before God in the midst of the church."

Gayle Gerber Koontz, "From a Distance" in Swartley, Mary and Rhoda Keener, eds. *She Has Done a Good Thing—Mennonite Women Leaders Tell Their Stories.* Scottsdale, PA: Herald Press, 1999, p. 35.

Boots and Cash

I stood in the used car lot slightly behind Bruce, fellow church member and mechanic. He was shaking the hand of the lot owner as the key to a used brown commercial van, with a seating capacity of fifteen, was dangled out for me to grab.

"Sure hope this van works out for you folks. It's got a few miles on it, but I hear it's for a good cause. Glad to help out. Now I need that $1,200. No checks allowed. Cash only."

The price had been wrangled out earlier in the lot as the two of us moved from used van to used van behind a heavy-set, greasy-panted dealer. I was along because, as the treasurer of a nonprofit inner-city school, I was authorizing the title to the school as owner. Bruce, a school supporter and obvious expert in all things motor, offered to help with a van search, engine expertise, and price negotiation. I had no experience with large vans, used car dealers, or price jockeying. My shoes were clean, my casual clothes an obvious sign of indoor work.

I was stunned. I had a check along ready to be made out for the final price. Bruce said, "Aw, come on! The check's legit."

"Sorry. No can do. I'll hold the keys while you get your cash."

We exited the shop and Bruce was stewing. "He's difficult." Enough said. Bruce drove to a bank where he had an account, muttering under his breath, and certain expletives escaped from time to time. "Sorry," he nodded in my direction, but neither of us were in the mood for conversation.

We stopped in front of the bank. Bruce told me to write out the check to him and he would cash it right then and there. We walked to the teller's window. "Hi Bruce," the friendly clerk announced. "How can I help you today?"

"Got a check to cash today—and I want it all in crisp, new ten-dollar bills."

"You want $1,200 in ten-dollar bills?"

"That's right."

The teller obliged, glancing at Bruce and me with a look that indicated to me that she had dealt with unusual requests from Bruce before. Bruce and I exited the bank and retraced our route to the used car lot. Just before we got out of the car, Bruce took the cash and stuffed all of it into his cowboy boots.

Again, I kept quiet.

We walked into the crude "office" where the cash register waited, and the dealer shuffled in from the lot. And with that, Bruce leaned over and pulled from his right boot a handful of ten-dollar bills. One by one, he counted them out loud until he retrieved the final $200 from the other boot. I probably gawked; the dealer stood mute as his hands began filling with cash. The deal was done.

"Thank you," I muttered as I took hold of a key chain and the title, now a sign of ownership.

The van proved reliable, and I took my turn driving unfamiliar streets to retrieve students who piled into the "brown beast" (as they called it).

I sometimes wonder how many other church parishioners had quirky skills for a good cause. As a pastor, I learned we need those folks.

Purple Hair

The beauty shop where Tiffany makes me look "super cute," a term I had never heard regarding a clergywoman's hairstyle, is a site of endless diversity. I make monthly appointments with her, the short-haired specialist in the shop, who sports a thick mass of purple hair full of unruly curls and over-the-eyes bangs. I never know exactly what she will do to me; however, she knows I'm a pastor and I must look "professional" (my word equivalency for her "super cute").

Nothing wags the tongues of parishioners as much as the clothing, hair, and jewelry of their female pastor. I discovered early in my career that what I wear, what jewelry I choose, and how I arrange my hair is fodder for parishioners. Everyone notices when I wear bright colors while preaching. Some remark, "Your earrings are pretty dangly!" And then there is the quizzical comment, "Did you get a perm?"

So, what's a female pastor to do? I determined over the past decades to find a Becky, or a Mary Lou, or a Tiffany—these women who know the shape of my head and the outline of my career. More than hairstyle, more than advice on hair products, these women connect me to the world.

Ironically, it's been my experience that the beauty shop is a place of community gatherings, pastoral care, and social gossip as vital as any congregation's inner workings. It's the place where I learn what's happening in the part of town I don't live in. It's the place where tidbits are shared about people who have a recent diagnosis of cancer or who are going through a "dadgum breakup from a sleaze-ball." It's the place where the foibles of a mother raising a teenage son with his father in prison and her live-in boyfriend "trying out fatherhood" is shared for pastoral advice.

"Say, Dorothy," Tiffany said one time. "Do you think there is a hell? I need to know because my friend, who's in the hospital, has never been to church. He's a good guy. Would God want him to burn in hell?" I shivered under my protective cape, waiting for my hair to dry and my mind to rev up a good, practical theological answer.

Once, an elderly man, clearly from the neighboring senior citizen high-rise, poked his head in the door. "Is this my day for a haircut?" he inquired.

The four stylists who were all in mid-stream of various clients' work, including mine, responded in nearly one voice, "Sure, Jimmy, come on in. Audrey will help you in a minute." He stepped inside, and I could see that his closely-shaved head did not need a haircut. No matter. He was treated with respect. Audrey helped him into her chair and announced, "We're going to make you handsome, Jimmy."

He grinned and asked, "Is this Thursday? I always come in on Thursday." Audrey assured him that he could come any day if he had the time!

Another day, as I sat waiting for my hair to turn away from graying (Tiffany's idea to "perk you up"), an elderly woman, bent over with osteoporosis, struggled to open the entry door. Instantly, two stylists rushed to door. "Just a minute, Norma. Let's get you safely inside." One stylist held the door, the other grabbed her cane and took her arm. Together they guided her to a waiting open chair, offering a pillow for her sit on, and then four helping hands lifted her safely onto the swivel chair.

"How's that? You comfortable?" It was clear this had happened before because Norma's driver simply stood outside and waited until her passenger was safely secured before going back to the waiting car.

I looked at the other clients: one was getting her hair turned red, white, and blue in a short summer cut; another was sitting with tight perm rollers; another was a young woman trying out an "updo" for her approaching wedding day.

Other times, men come in talking of business plans, building codes, girlfriend's closets, and trucks that need new tires. Giggly little girls, grasping their toy dolls, and tearful little boys, grimacing as they got their heads shaved, were escorted in by tired-looking moms and grandmas tasked with getting the kids their haircuts.

But every time I sit in the chair, I observe a community of differing ages, abilities, and social class. There is diversity, welcome, care, and service. How I wish that congregations were as welcoming and diverse as Tiffany's place. Purple hair might just be the ticket to visible signs of creativity and welcome. Meanwhile, I sit waiting to be "super cute."

How to Say Hello and Goodbye with Joy

It never fails. Each generation claims there is a gap, and it seems to exist in the church as well. What shall we do with our young adults? How can we communicate? Will they keep the faith? Or, as I like to say, will the faith keep them?

After living and serving in congregations where university-related individuals were involved in the church and its mission, I have observed several things.

1. Be prepared to win—and to lose

People who are heavily involved in college or graduate school are busy but also thirsty for support. Often, congregations and church communities can be that vital link between a demanding school schedule that drains precious energy in academic rigor and an urgent yearning for connections to a spiritual home.

Congregations "win" when they offer a church home to young adults. They will be blessed with the "best and the brightest." They will receive the talents (sometimes hidden for a bit) of music, dramatic arts, nurturing child care, stimulating conversation, theological inquisitiveness, and budding church leadership. It is a golden moment of discovering gifts that will be used in the church setting.

But the congregations may "lose," too. Sporadic schedules, the demands of exams and dissertations, travel plans, and decisions to change programs will result in irregular attendance, lack of consistency in the ongoing life of the church, and sometimes irreconcilable choices of time for research and time for church. This can lead to disappointment for both the congregation and the individual.

The key is understanding that young adults are in a time of intense training that has little tolerance for divided loyalties. But for those who choose to share their lives with a local congregation, the rewards are mutual.

2. Watch for widening horizons—and for narrowing ones

Just as the mind begins to open to new possibilities as knowledge is learned, so do the life choices that young adults can make. Choices unheard of even a decade ago become new career and degree tracks. As these many opportunities beckon, the world becomes a stage. Some students, for example, have never lived anywhere but home. They are exposed to people from other cities and other countries in this new academic context. They hear about different religions, see moral issues from other points of view, and are often overwhelmed with the freedom to choose their activities. This expanding horizon is exhilarating and energizing. They find themselves and claim identities.

But for some, this seemingly endless platter of choices is too much. They are overwhelmed. They choose foolishly. They decide that being different from Mom and Dad is better than careful thinking. They leap without looking. Sometimes they drop out of the church because that is too conservative a thing to be part of. It wouldn't be thinkable to be in a conventional church setting, especially on a Sunday morning, after being quite unconventional on Saturday night. And so, the horizons narrow—and the young adult skips the spiritual diet of congregational life for the more typical peer lifestyle that has long since dropped out of church.

3. Watch for the academic giant in religious kindergarten

One of the more fascinating discoveries I made when ministering to and with young adults was their virtual endless quest for academic rigor in their chosen discipline. Students are on the cutting edge of new research, designing new applications to ancient problems, and delving into detailed analysis of documents.

However, I also discovered, these same students are often not ready to subject their own faith or religious understandings to scrutiny. New ideas in religion can be threatening or seen as unnecessary. Sometimes students seek comfort from religion (not unlike the majority of Sunday morning attendees). They simply want to be reassured about the basics of their faith and not worry about thorny ethical dilemmas or church politics at the summer conference. Tradition is important—but only at church.

Gently leading young adults along the path of faith is rewarding, but it must be done carefully and prayerfully. The life cycle of testing and searching often occurs at this same time of being in a university-related congregation. Walking along with them is rewarding, even if exasperating. The possibilities of engaging these individuals in a deepening spiritual vision are endless. Most are grateful that you are there to try the new, challenge the traditional, and open doors to new thinking. But don't be shocked by the ones who say, "I want church to be a place of rest—not thinking."

4. Be prepared to walk on holy ground—and in the depths of hell

One of the greatest joys for me as pastor, especially in a university-related congregation, was the chance to participate in the life choices of many individuals. This involved vocational decisions, choosing marriage partners, birthing first babies, deciding on baptism, and making major independent life choices.

The possibility of baptizing a new Christian who could say to me, "Dorothy, that Jesus was a radical. He turned the world upside down. I want to follow Him," was truly breathtaking. The joy of doing premarital counseling with couples making lifelong commitments was there. The dedication of a new child with admiring parents amid a supportive congregation was a holy moment. The ability to challenge congregational members to welcome the new student, the new resident, the international visitor, over and over again, was inspiring. To mark the major life directions in the context of the church was truly a sacred trust.

However, there were the agonies of decisions that forced painful choices. I was there to witness the roommates who turned into stiff competitors for scholarships. I saw the grief of losing a first grandparent to death and being unable to attend the funeral because it conflicted with the only exam for a class. I heard the depression that turned so deep that suicide seemed the only choice. I listened to the stories of injury and abuse that many had suffered in their homes and families. The depths of hell are part of the pastoring and congregational ministry when relating to young adults.

5. Remember that your future pastor, conference executive, or church planter may be sitting in the back row this next Sunday

The opportunity for the university-related congregation to mentor new leaders for church ministry is never-ending. Eager minds plus idealism equals opportunities for the seeds of ministry to be planted.

I was often the one who asked questions like: What is in your future? Have you ever considered voluntary service? Would you like to see the world and serve humanity at the same time? Can you invent a machine that will aid the farmers of the world? Are you able to design a building that can meet the needs of the aging? Will you find the chemical equation that will cure cancer?

These and other questions are not academic when you minister to young adults. These students are wrestling with life's largest problems. And they just may find the solutions.

To include service to others as part of their vocational and academic preparation is part of the church's challenge to young adults. Getting involved in a congregation that keeps the inward and outward components of the gospel ever-present challenges these participants to use their skills in the service of the church. What a privilege!

6. Learn to say hello and goodbye with grace

The most enjoyable part of ministry in a university-related congregation is the multitude of hellos. Every September, a new church is planted. Who will be there? What new faces will appear? Will last year's faithful show up?

And they come—eager yet anxious, conservative and liberal, Mennonite and "other than Mennonite," young and slightly older, mostly on borrowed money, casual, and generally looking for a friend. They offer to teach Sunday school, serve on the worship committee, staff the nursery, sing a solo, play the piano or guitar or drums, fix your car, bake bread, and interrupt your day with a friendly, "Are you busy?" Church for the year is based on who shows up.

But there are the inevitable goodbyes. No program lasts forever. People graduate, find jobs, and move away. Those are the expected partings. Worse, they fail exams, have dissertations rejected, or get fired or downsized and must leave. Those are awkward and wrenching partings. When you have invested in these lives and given even a few minutes in a special way, it is hard to say goodbye.

Learning to walk alongside these students, faculty, and staff members is a lesson in grace and humility. Unpredictability and change are constant. The ministry of hospitality, of welcoming, and of opening the heart and soul to new people in the church is of absolute necessity to minister in this situation. Learning to say goodbye with tears and an aching heart is also a discipline. Sending and commissioning people to the next stop in their life journey are equally satisfying and necessary in the life of the church.

Ministry in the university-related congregation is an extraordinary challenge and reward. Knowing that God is there, preparing women and men to learn and serve, is a source of comfort and challenge as we face the future.

Hot Bean Juice Communion

We were tramping in the hilly fields in Northwestern Brazil in late March. The morning was marked with warm sun and gracious farmers. Our guide was a woman, maybe in her '70s, who walked too fast for most of the nine North Americans who were following her unmarked path.

We started near the schoolhouse and proceeded up a windy path, through the small plots of beans and corn. Suddenly, we were at her home surveying a large shed. She pointed to the pile of manioc lying on the ground. Tubers resembling sweet potatoes were stacked three feet high in front of a press. Proudly, she cranked the small engine to demonstrate the operation, but it repeatedly sputtered and died.

Finally, her husband, who had been watching this motley group of foreigners from the safety of his porch, came to give his hand to the crank. His bare back was leathery and a deep bronze color. With his simple, quick action, the motor came to life, and our group cheered his accomplishments. She said, "I primed it well!" in Portuguese, and we laughed when the translator told us her quip.

We saw how the manioc was pressed, then processed in a huge open vat over fire, and then ground into manioc flour. The process involved back-breaking work from start to finish. All the work was mostly done by hand—from bending over to dig the manioc, to lifting pails of pressed mush, to stirring over a hot cauldron, to pounding into flour. The entire family, from young children to grandparents, was involved in the process; all were thin and wiry in stature.

"Would you like to see my house?" Of course, we wanted to see her home, and so we tramped farther up the hill. The simple structure had four rooms, a red tile roof, a dirt floor, and few furnishings. Windows were protected with bars but no screens. A small stove, a table, several chairs, an old couch, and a bed were the only pieces of furniture.

"Would you like to taste my beans?" Of course, we would be pleased to taste her food. She found plastic glasses of assorted colors and sizes and poured a small amount of hot red bean juice into each one. We could hardly hold the glasses because of the boiling contents, but we sipped the tangy mixture. She shared with everyone, offering second helpings to the brave. This, no doubt, represented her supper meal and maybe even several meals, but she kept dipping into the simmering bean pot, offering more and more and more.

We slowly exited her home with repeated thanks. A few chickens ran freely; a dog and several scrawny kittens played in the sunshine. It was then that I saw the zinnias. Very neatly around her front door were rows of zinnias.

When we North Americans traveled to Brazil to visit Mennonite Central Committee project sites, we saw urban and rural situations that overwhelmed us. Poverty is pervasive; conditions are sparse; basic necessities are lacking. We struggled with questions of justice and of hope. We analyzed the systems of farming, marketing, and consuming. Yet, we saw evidence of incredible strength amidst overwhelming odds. Beauty knows no income level. Intentional flower-planting became a symbol of survival and of adornment. Hot bean juice was a modern-day wine of communion.

That is what serving in the name of Christ is like. We become neighbors with strangers as we share potlucks or summer lemonade. And so, even now, I will keep looking for zinnias in North America, too.

You Just Gotta' Laugh—Six Stories

Piano player: There were only twenty-two of us in the congregation that Sunday where I was the guest preacher. The pianist was a member of another congregation but came to play at the Mennonite congregation twice a month. This was her Sunday. She obviously did not know the opening hymn, as we struggled through verse one at a slow pace with many incorrect notes. She called out, "Don't know this one. Give me a chance." Verse two went a little faster and more accurately. As we started verse three, she announced from the piano bench, "I'm getting this one." We made it through without obvious clunkers. By verse four, she shared, "Sure glad we have four verses so I could learn this one." We finished the hymn—all the verses.

Worship leader: The worship leader stepped up to the pulpit, pulled out some notes from his shirt pocket, and said, "Good morning. Glad you're here. Got a guest speaker here, and I'll try not to mess things up." He then announced the opening hymn—which was not the one printed in the bulletin. The organist shouted out the correct hymn number. He waved at her and leaned into the microphone to announce her correction. We sat down, and he started to read the Sunday's scripture—again different from the bulletin. Finally, he turned to me, the guest speaker, and said, "I'm not sure what's going on." I, as guest speaker on the platform, then gave him my bulletin, and he said, "Guess I had last week's bulletin in my pocket. Here we go with the right stuff."

Guest preacher: As the guest preacher, I was walking to the platform with the worship leader at the beginning of the service. As the organist finished the prelude, nothing happened. The worship leader did not stand. I did not stand. I looked at the bulletin and finally surmised that the preacher was the "stander" and "sitter" in this congregation. As a guest, I had no idea what to do. Finally, I stood up. The congregation followed, and I simply guessed at the rituals for the rest of the service. As I left the service, one woman said, "Nice sermon, but we really popped up a lot. Guess you like to stand to sing hymns."

Communion bread: My eyes were nearly closed in prayer as I led the congregation in the celebration of communion. We had left the front doors open for the lovely fall day. The communion table was stocked with a freshly baked loaf of bread and two goblets of grape juice. Everything was set when in walked a cat. I saw the movement and noted all people in the front row had their eyes closed in prayer—except one usher. The cat was inching closer and closer and was ready to pounce when a front-row man leapt forward, catching the cat just as it prepared for a fresh bread breakfast. I prayed as he exited with the cat, and few parishioners ever knew of the near holy food catastrophe.

Barking dog: Our meeting place was the rented large open space of a campus ministries building. Each Sunday, the Mennonites set up folding chairs, added a banner in the front, and moved the piano into position. The building also had a large kitchen, several offices, and an apartment where student custodians lived—a trade for rent. One Sunday, as I started to preach, a dog started barking in the apartment. Evidently, the college student had gone out for breakfast and left his dog (not allowed in the lease) alone. The dog, now needing attention, heard our voices and singing and promptly started his chorus of barking. Amidst the giggling and smiling, and then irritated faces, our congregation listened as I preached with periodic barking. Finally, the custodian ran in from the front door and we heard the apartment door open and shut. Silence. No one remembered a thing about the sermon.

Taxi prayer: "Pastor, you got to pray for me." The older man was a regular mid-morning chat at our church in the inner city. He drove a taxi and used our church's corner location as a place for finding riders. "Sure," I said. "Anything special?" He replied, "Yup! You gotta pray that my new paint color will be the right shade of yellow." So I held his hand as we stood by his car. He put his hand on the front hood, head raised heavenward, eyes closed. I prayed, *"God, please bless Harry and his taxi business. And today, bless the painter, too. Amen."*

"Thank you, preacher. Sure glad for your connections."

CHAPTER 6

Sacred Encounters

"O Heroine of heroines, Your wisdom is reflected in the stories of our sisters and Your power is made manifest in the outlines of their lives. You were there when they stood for justice and You rode with them into battle against all the evil forces that surrounded and still surround. Be with us now as we too face the hour of our decision. Make us strong, secure, confident that You will achieve what we must do. We praise Your name, and we thank You in the name of all women. Amen."

Winter, Miriam Therese. *Woman Witness—A Feminist Lectionary and Psalter; Women of the Hebrew Scriptures: Part Two*, New York: Crossroad Publishing, 1992, p. 107.

Long-Sleeved Visitor

I watched her leave my office, turn slowly, and walk with her head down toward the exit. As she pushed the door, she deftly pulled the headscarf over her head and wrapped the long cloth around her neck. She never appears in public without her hijab.

I sat down at my desk and pondered my next step. Do I call the university's student services division and report that a man is severely depressed and will not leave his apartment, as his wife just reported?

I dialed the office of the woman who referred Nadia to me in the first place.

"Hello, Maxine," I began. "Wanted to get back to you about that referral you sent my way."

"Do you mean Nadia? So glad for your quick response. She seemed very distraught and wanted to talk with a religious person—a woman! I couldn't think of anyone except you. Thanks again for your efforts."

My good colleague Maxine had called earlier in the semester and asked, "What do you know about cross-cultural counseling?"

"Not too much. Why do you ask?" had been my quick reply. But I agreed to meet Nadia for a first time.

Now, months later, I recalled that first meeting.

Nadia was a beautiful woman—tall, dark-eyed, slender. Her blouse had flowing long sleeves and her skirt draped over her slim figure. Her sense of style, her gracefulness, and her appropriately elegant jewelry all sent a message of confidence, maybe even wealth.

After the polite initial greeting, Nadia respectfully requested an hour of my time to discuss her vocational future. She was graduating in May with a master's degree and was in the job market. Would San Francisco or St. Paul be a better place to live?

So that was it. She needed vocational counseling and help sorting out her options. No problem, I thought. This I can do.

That first conversation ended as politely as it had begun. Nadia left—agreeing to see me in a couple of weeks when she had finished her first round of interviewing. I was more than a bit puzzled—since I had seen no hint of distress. No tears, no agitation, no trauma. Just the usual anxiety that graduates face in numerous interviews and job searches. Trying, yes. Exhausting, yes. But really nothing out of the ordinary.

Maxine, eager for a report, called me later that day. "Did she show up? What did she say? I know you really can't tell me, but is everything all right?"

"You better cool it, Maxine. There's nothing wrong. She simply needs a listening ear as she figures out which job she will take."

"But what about her arm? Did she show it to you?"

I was stunned into silence.

"Her arm?" I meekly responded.

"Yes, her arm. It was in a sling yesterday. Seems she fell. But I doubt it. I think something happened at home. I can't believe you didn't notice it."

"Maxine, there was no sling. She wore a beautiful long-sleeved blouse. She never said anything. In fact, she didn't even mention if she was married or anything. I was hesitant to ask too many questions—that cross-cultural thing is something I was conscious of. I'm sure that the Arab women are less 'up front' than North Americans. Maxine, I think I missed something."

During the next several months, Nadia appeared mostly regularly every other week. And bit by bit, I uncovered a frightened and battered woman. The beautiful clothes were carefully chosen to cover bruise marks. On one occasion, Nadia limped into my office. She shyly pulled her dress up to uncover a purple bruise the size of a football on her thigh.

"What happened?" I asked in horror.

"I fell," she began. Then she put her head in her hands and began a silent weeping.

I waited.

"You are a fine Christian woman. I am a new Christian—but I wear the hijab out of respect for my parents and my Muslim teachings. I became a Christian this spring, hoping that a new religion would help me at home. My husband sits all day on the sofa or stays in bed. He keeps the curtains drawn and doesn't allow our son to go out and play after school. He is very depressed because he finished his PhD and can't find a job. He has lots of money and wants me to be his queen. But I had my school work, and now

I am finished. I want to find a job. He says we can move back to Kuwait or Iraq! I hated it there. I couldn't even work there—it wouldn't be allowed!"

The story tumbled out that day and led to an intriguing relationship with Nadia. Sometimes, she would drop in like a silent cat. I would offer a cup of tea and a listening ear while she sat on the edge of the upholstered chair as if she could spring up quickly and be gone. I also made very sure she understood that I was a Christian, not a Muslim, and that I was considered a clergyperson—leading a church. Our congregation even gave her one hundred dollars from its Compassion Fund so she could fill out application forms. She assured us she would repay it when she got a job—which was not a requirement from us.

"That's why I visit with you," she pleaded. "My other pastor told me that suffering like Jesus is what being a Christian is all about. He told me to pray more and to be sure I dressed properly. He even thought that I might think of quitting school to be with my husband more. I think that's why Maxine wanted me to talk with you. She said that not all Christians agree about some things. Your culture is hard for me to understand sometimes. Are Mennonites different than other churches?"

I found few words that day to explain the difference between Mennonites and her church, the role of suffering in faith, different views on women's roles, and the meaning of marriage. All of that seemed entirely too complicated and yet so basic.

So, when we met that day, I saw her leave for the last time. She decided to take that job in Minnesota, moving with her son and leaving her husband in Kansas. She thought she probably wouldn't stay a Christian because I hadn't really helped her. She had lost a husband. "But," she said at that last conversation, "He didn't kill me like they did Jesus."

And then I moved away. I had a new job in another state. I tried to leave a message for her, but the phone call was never answered. I lost touch with Nadia, an immigrant living in the cocoon of the university system.

It was nearly twenty years later, as I had moved twice more and now lived back in Kansas, that my administrative assistant at the Western District Conference office told me that I had a call from a woman named Nadia who wanted my address, so she could send me money that I had loaned her. "I think this is a fraud, so I didn't give out any information."

I groaned. "No, no. This is legit! You could not have known. She is someone from my past. Do you have any information?"

There was no information, and I worried and pined for Nadia's friendship.

About a year later, a similar phone call came to my conference office. Again, I was out, and Nadia never left any contact information. We tried to trace the phone call, but the number was disconnected.

To this day, I still wonder if she is wearing long-sleeved blouses.

Demons

I was vaguely aware of demon possession and religious deliverance ministry when I lived in northern Indiana. A local Mennonite man there specialized in caring for victims of demon possession, and some other Mennonite pastors and leaders served as an accountability group on behalf of the area denomination's conference. As an administrative faculty member at the Mennonite seminary, I encountered both support and downright hostility to this specialized ministry. I was extremely suspicious—especially when most of his clientele were women.

I was later pastoring in Kansas when a phone call came from that same northern Indiana minister who specialized in deliverance ministry. He had a national reputation for his knowledge and experience with people deemed demon possessed.

"I don't think you know me, but you and I met at a conference on deliverance ministries some years ago here in northern Indiana."

"Why yes, I remember you," I responded. "I know of your ministry, and I am now a pastor in a university city."

"Well, that's why I am calling you. Do you have some time for this call? It could take some explanation."

And, with that, I learned that he wanted to make a referral of a woman who had been in residence with him and was now healed of demon possession. He wanted me to do follow-up pastoral care.

"She is quite fragile, but I think the worst is past. She made remarkable progress, and we were able to deliver nearly a dozen demons from her. It is quite a hard case, and I want her to see a woman pastor in Manhattan—her home town. Are you able to meet with her?"

I struggled to respond. This was way out of my league! My gut turned crampy and I was lost for words.

Immediately, my mind raced back to my seminary leadership experience with international students objecting to a campus-wide Halloween event that I was orchestrating as part of my student life portfolio.

"What?" the seminary student from Argentina exploded. "You are hosting a Halloween party? That's evil. We don't want the spirits released on campus."

And with that, I was bombarded by furious and frightened international students who viewed Halloween parties—complete with costumes, games, and treats—as participating in the underground of demon possession. I, on the other hand, thought that organizing a family event on campus would be fun. What could be wrong with kids trick or treating? Who wouldn't like games like bobbing for apples and treats like cupcakes and orange punch?

However, these vocal students, especially, recounted experiences, in detail, of chairs moving across the room in their grandparents' living room, of people speaking strange languages, and of bodies contorted as convulsions gripped otherwise healthy neighbors. I was surely respectful of their religious perspective and a bit embarrassed for hosting a party that seemed downright dangerous to them.

"Of course, I would not host an event that in any way invited evil on our campus. Halloween trick or treating is a ritual of fun and neighborhood tradition in the US. I thought that many of our residents and families would appreciate staying on campus yet also enjoying a party. You do not have to participate, and we will make clear that this is a national custom and meant for entertainment only."

The damage, however, was done. The whole event was plagued by misunderstanding and pitted international students against North American students. I was culturally insensitive. I hurt my relationships with several students, and my social and entrepreneurial self took a hit. Were there evil spirits that haunted families? Had our students experienced a spirituality that I did not understand?

"Are you still there?" he queried.

"Yes, I am still here, but I am stunned by your request. To be honest, I'm not sure I am qualified to do this work. Shouldn't she be in professional counseling? Is she Mennonite? Is she even open to talking with me?"

What followed was a convincing request to give her a call and try to arrange an appointment. If she came, fine. If not, then I would simply let him know. Nothing more was required.

Was I again being sucked into a situation where my caring self was being tested? Were evil spirits part of my ministry? What would my congregation say if they knew I was dealing with demon possession? Well, I knew what most of them would say—and it would not be positive or supportive. I was feeling alone, ill-equipped yet strangely responsible. Was pastoral ministry about compassion? I recalled my boundaries of professional training, and I would surely be careful.

"I am so hesitant, but I will contact her, and I will let you know when and if we meet. I will certainly document any conversation."

With that, we exchanged phone numbers and addresses and agreed to keep each other informed if there was any contact by either of us with Marilyn.

I put the phone down and proceeded to dial her number—not expecting much. She answered and surprisingly said, "Yes, I am glad to meet with you. I was promised a local pastor, and Pastor Glen said someone would call me. Yes, I will see you. Is today possible?" Shocked by her eagerness to meet, I agreed to a late-afternoon appointment in my office.

Marilyn was a frail-looking woman. She wore clothes that were modest and casual—probably a size from when she weighed much more. Her green long-sleeved sweater hung on her, and the simple blouse and skirt seemed dated. Her shyness and quiet voice were hard to read. After all, I was a total stranger. And a Mennonite—what did she know about my religion? My occupation?

The conversation was not easy as I asked simple questions about her family, her education, and lots of "get acquainted" type inquiries. She gave short answers and looked exhausted. Finally, she said, "I am still pretty sick. The spirits keep trying to confuse me. I hear them all the time, but there aren't so many now."

I realized right then and there that she needed professional help—maybe even hospitalization. I was totally frightened by her confession. What did she expect from me?

"You should pray for me," she volunteered after some silence. "That always helps."

I could pray! Of course! I reached out to hold her hands in mine, and she immediately responded with a smile and outstretched hands. She seemed relieved to make contact.

I prayed a simple prayer reminding her that she was made in God's image and that God loved her. I probably slipped in something about "other helpers in Manhattan who would also be available" since I knew I could not and would not keep this relationship mine alone. (Sometimes prayers are public information disguised as spiritual language.) *"Be merciful, O God, and bring healing and hope to Marilyn."*

She left and promised to call me again for another appointment. I told her I would make a contact with a counselor at the local mental health center to assist her in feeling better.

The next call did not come from her but from her husband. "Would you please meet with me? I need to give you some background before you meet with Marilyn again."

Jeff was a middle-aged man who was grateful for a chance to talk with me. His worn blue jeans, faded flannel shirt, and cowboy boots were confirmation that he was a rancher as Marilyn had told me.

"It's been a long journey. Our recent trip to northern Indiana was the most recent of many trips to faith-healers in the country. She is so convinced that demons are in her head and that if we just find the right pastor, she will get better. She has been to lots of therapists and taken lots of medications, but she never follows up and never takes the meds for very long. And then the cycle starts all over. She lets me drive so I can be with her, but she sometimes suggests she will just get in the car and drive where the spirits tell her to go. I'm afraid she'll drive into the ditch or a river or even have an accident. What if she rams into somebody thinking they are a spirit? I've lost my school janitor job because I must take care of her. We're out of money. I can still take care of our small farm, but I don't know what to do. Will you help me?"

Now I had two needy people! Marilyn and Jeff were caught in a cycle of ill health, mercy ministries, and repeated cycles of mental illness. I was now upset with Pastor Glen, who did not inform me of Marilyn's long history of demon possession, faith-healers, and family struggles.

I agreed with Jeff that he needed care and support. I was willing to meet with him (and with Marilyn) only if he (and she) were in professional counseling. I found out that their adult children had stopped visiting them and that their church family had burned out in caring for them. They were alone and desperate. Jeff admitted he was ready to divorce Marilyn or commit her to a mental hospital. "She won't go, and she will hate me forever. I couldn't do that. I'm a Christian."

"Jeff, being a Christian means you must do some things so your wife gets the right help. Chasing around the country is not working. Marilyn needs psychiatric care now. We have a wonderful facility right here in Manhattan, and I have arranged a consultation with a therapist." I handed him the card from a mental health colleague that I had met with—plus a card from the mental health chaplain who also had assured me she could assist this family.

He had tears in his eyes and suggested that I not meet with Marilyn anymore. "She just goes from person to person. I don't think that will help. You are very kind, but I don't think this is a good idea. You are right. We must try therapy again. Thanks." He heaved a deep sigh, stood up, shook my hand, and left.

I sat at my desk, put my head in my hands, and wept. The tragedy of mental illness, the long journey of seeking help, the spiritual struggles, and the loss of relationships—including mine—seemed a sad, sad helping of grief.

I sent a brief letter to the referral from Indiana: "Dear Glen: It is my humble opinion that Marilyn needs a specially trained pastor plus a psychiatrist, social worker, family counselor, and medical doctor. I am not qualified in this work. I have referred her to professionals in our community."

Marilyn never called me again. I did get a notice that Jeff had made an appointment for himself at the community mental health center. My pastoral care connection with them was over.

Eager Volunteers

September

I sat in my office after ushering out three young college students. They were polite and eager to volunteer at our church. We desperately needed a youth teacher for the fall semester.

"You see, we are friends that arrived here to go to graduate school in education. We need to find an internship with youth as part of our first semester's assignment. We thought that volunteering in a church would be a good experience."

"Of course," I echoed. "We have a small youth group, and they would be great to work with. Tell me a bit about yourselves and what you know about Mennonites."

The answers were vague, and then they admitted, "We don't know anything about Mennonites, but they're Christians, right?"

I wondered just how much time I would have to devote to supervision of these volunteers and how three university students would connect with our ten junior and senior high youth. What would be the curriculum? What would we do about service trips? What about volunteering in local nonprofits? What did they know about me, the pastor? Why the Mennonite church? The questions just kept on coming.

Finally, I said, "Let's do this. Please join us for worship next Sunday where you will have a chance to meet the youth, their parents, and other people who are part of our fellowship. After that visit, you will have a better understanding of who we are. Let's meet the following week, and we can design the future."

It was a plan with the possibility of incorporating some new young adults into our church.

They never showed up for worship—that next Sunday or ever. I forgot about them.

November

The fall semester moved along and, as usual, I attended the local Ministerial Association's monthly meeting. One ritual was the sharing time during lunch. "What's happening? What's 'hot' in your church?" After that personal sharing, we had a session of prayer and then a slew of announcements about events, projects, and community concerns.

I enjoyed the fellowship and the genuine cooperation I felt. Also, through this network of pastors, our congregation got connected with other congregations for activities like a film series or a summer church softball league. We even took our turn by hosting a rice and beans supper featuring concerns about Central American refugees. Ecumenical relationships were important, and I was thrilled to be included in a mostly male leadership circle.

As we went around the circle, the local Baptist church's lead pastor took his turn. "Folks, I need to share a deep concern. I think our youth program has been hijacked!" With that, he went into the story of three university students who came to his office in early September describing a needed internship for an education course at the university.

My ears perked up, and I quickly offered, "They visited me, too—but they never returned despite my suggestion to attend worship at our fellowship, so I didn't follow up with them."

"Lucky you didn't!" retorted the pastor. In short, the three students had been invited by the pastor to teach their high school youth Sunday school class. "You know how hard it is to get anyone to take on that group!" We all nodded and exchanged weary glances.

"Well, after about three weeks, one of our students told his parents that the three students were great and 'excited' about teaching, but the lessons were about world religions. I said that I thought some learning about religions in the world was a good thing, especially in a university town. I had (vaguely) approved the curriculum that the three said they were developing. However, in some casual conversations with other parents and their teenagers, I began to hear that every lesson was about the Unification Church. They're Moonies!"

With that, we stopped eating our salads and stared at the Baptist pastor.

"They're recruiting our youth to be part of THEIR church!"

After a stunned silence, another pastor offered that the three had come to his office as they had to mine, offering to teach youth. He reported they were set for the fall and never bothered to ask anything further.

The Presbyterian pastor, a bold leader of the largest Protestant congregation in the community, said something like, "Don't you folks have any screening for volunteers? Applications? References?"

His smug chiding was deserved. It was clear that all of us needed to step up our policies for "hiring" volunteers, just as most of us did for paid staff. As a Ministerial Association, we then prayed for each other—and invoked the Holy Spirit to prod us toward wise decisions.

War's Prisoner

He knocked on the church office door but would not enter after the administrative assistant motioned for him to enter. He knocked again, and she went to the door and invited him in.

"No, I want the pastor," he said and pointed to the stairs.

She came into my office. "You're needed out here. It's Helmut. He's our member—but not sure what's going on."

After a bit of confusing instructions, I followed Helmut into the hallway and down the steps to the outside entrance. There, parked right in front of the church, was his car. It was old, and one of the doors was clearly mismatched from the others. There were decals plastered over all sides, and an American flag waved from the back window. "Give peace a chance" and "Buy American" were slogans amidst crosses, Bibles, and praying hands.

"See," he said as he moved me toward the passenger side door. "It's about you!"

I looked carefully. There, in script, was Isaiah 40:31: "*. . .but those who wait for the Lord shall renew their strength, they shall mount up with wings like eagles, they shall run and not be weary, they shall walk and not faint.*"

"See," he said again. "This is your favorite Bible verse. It's mine, too! You said last Sunday it was your favorite. Now I know you were sent to my church. See, my car has proof!"

And, with that, I began to learn about and from Helmut over the next years.

Helmut was born in Poland and then joined the occupying German army in World War II. He was captured by the Americans and sent to a Prisoner of War camp in the United States—near Chicago. During his imprisonment, he longed to be back in Germany and escaped the camp. He was hunted down and put in confinement, where he deteriorated. He was freed at the end of WWII. Through federal government assistance, he could settle in the United States and bring his wife from Germany. Eventually, they were resettled in our community. His wife was a gracious, long-suffering woman with a thick German accent and plump figure. They had three American-born children.

However, over the years, Helmut "heard" things, saw designs in the sky, and believed messages were being sent through his teeth that he was being hunted. The whole town knew of his mental illness—but the whole town also knew that Helmut had suffered horribly in his life.

During worship, he always sat on the east side of the congregation, just beneath the giant stained-glass window picturing Jesus knocking on the door. "They can't find me here." He often put aluminum foil over the hymnal rack in front of him to "stop the messages" from invading his mind. He was welcomed by other parishioners. I'm sure parents needed to assure their children that Helmut was their friend even though he acted strangely and mumbled at times.

His physical body weakened, and he developed skin cancer on his face. He refused treatment because he was convinced the doctors would give him poison—not medicine. Finally, a doctor in our congregation managed to treat Helmut tenderly, but his physical health declined; he needed to move to nursing care. Helmut died, and the whole congregation filled the sanctuary giving thanks for his life, recalling his reputation for pointing out political foibles by the government (even at the pharmacy or in the aisles of the supermarket). We released Helmut to eternal life and wholeness.

Helmut was a prisoner of war, but he also captured our community with his presence. He became an object, to some, of the disease of mental illness; but to others, he was a symbol of survival and endurance. His family loved him, his church accepted him, and Jesus stood over him every Sunday.

Some Will Con You

I had just finished eating my Sunday lunch of pancakes when the phone rang.

"I have a collect call for the pastor of the Mennonite Church from Ken Coblentz. Will you accept the charge?"

"Yes, I will."

"This is a call for the pastor."

"I am the pastor."

"Oh, excuse me, ma'am. Go ahead." (Operator goes off the line.)

"Praise the Lord! Praise the Lord! I found a Mennonite pastor!"

"May I help you? Is there something you need?"

"Praise the Lord! I'm in terrible trouble. I've got a lot of problems. I knew you would be able to help. You see, I'm here in Solomon, Kansas, at a truck stop."

"Solomon? Just where is that? I'm new here, so don't know my towns really well."

"Just fourteen miles east of Salina. You see, I hitched a ride with a trucker here, and now I'm waiting for a ride home, but I have only sixty-two cents and really need some money. I've been in an accident and my wife's back got broken, and now we're on our way to Edmonton, Alberta, which is home."

"You are a long way from home. When did the accident happen?"

"Oh, last week. You see, I'm an ex-Amish man, and well, you might say I'm the black sheep of the family. I ran away and became a truck driver. You know, one of those eighteen-wheeler kinds? I think the Lord is trying to tell me something. You see, I was in Florida and I was driving my truck when a school bus came out of nowhere, and I had a choice to make: either go off the interstate overpass I was on or hit a bus with little kids. I managed to stop the truck by jack-knifing it, but I really got hurt and so did my wife,

Mary. I've seen the light. I'm going back to my community. But it's a long way away.

"What do you need the money for?"

"A bus ticket home. I've got a ride to the Canadian border, and then I need to buy a ticket to get home, which costs $165. I can't call my pastor, Roger Hochstetler, at home because he doesn't have a phone. It's against their religion, you know. Now I need the money quick 'cause this trucker is about to leave and we have to go along."

"I'm surprised your wife is traveling. I thought she had a broken back."

"Well, we're not sure it's broken. It's swollen real bad and pretty red. But we couldn't afford a full body cast, so we just decided to try to get home and then we'll take care of it."

"Well, I don't think I can get $165 to you at all. You are calling Manhattan, which is quite a bit farther away from the truck stop than Salina is. Have you tried to get help from someone there?"

"Yes, ma'am, I did. The Salvation Army says we're not in bad enough shape, and so we didn't get any help."

"What about the police? They sometimes know of agencies that help people passing through."

"Look! I haven't broken the law."

"I didn't say you had. But sometimes the police can offer help in emergency situations. That's what they're there for."

"Well, we really need the money. If you could wire me the money, I'd be very grateful. I could even do some work to pay you back."

"What kind of work do you do?"

"Well, it would have to be quite a while down the road. You see, I got hurt pretty bad in the accident, so the doctor says I can't do anything for a long time."

"I suggest you call someone in Salina. I just don't have that kind of money. Our church is a small fellowship. Does your home church know you need help? Does your family realize you are hurt? Maybe they could wire you the money."

"I have no way of contacting them."

"You do have a ride to the Canadian border. That gets you much closer to home. Maybe you should take this ride and keep on going."

"Yes, you're probably right. I haven't eaten and I'm real hungry. But I thank you for listening."

"I'm sorry I can't be of more help. I hope your life gets better. Maybe going home will be the best thing."

"I sure hope so. Thank you. God bless you. Goodbye."

"Goodbye."

Later that week, I contacted Rev. Roger Hochstetler in Edmonton, Alberta, whose name my caller had mentioned. He has never heard of a Ken Goblentz. I was the fifth person to call him and ask about an ex-Amish man needing money. The calls have come from Kansas, Texas, and Louisiana from pastors of Mennonite churches as well as one from a Nazarene pastor. The story from one person was different: he now needed $180 and was going to start dairy farming in Alberta.

Sometimes in this charity work there are a few con men. But, we can, in the last analysis, never know when the voice asking for help is the voice of Christ needing food, water, or shelter. This time, my only cost was a collect phone call.

Excuse me, I hear my phone ringing.

Prison Visit

"Have you ever been in prison?" was the question from my traveling companion as I maneuvered the car through traffic near Omaha, Nebraska. We were getting close to the federal penitentiary.

"Heavens no!" came my quick reply. I regretted the words as soon as they were out of my mouth. Why hadn't I protested like her spouse had? I was a committed pacifist, too. He had spilled his blood on the steps of the local post office steps on April 15. He protested the taxes that went to war. Public witness was, literally, in his blood. Our congregation supported him, and now I, as his pastor and friend, was going to visit him in prison because of his nonviolent action. His sentence was short—twelve weeks—but that seemed incredibly long to me.

"This is certainly no fun for me," she mused. "But I knew this was going to happen. He is so sure that public witness is important. I support him, and we decided I would not join him that day since we have kids to take care of."

"Of course," I added quickly. "You are doing the right thing. You are just as committed to peace as he is."

We fell into silence as she coached me from her map about turns, parking lots, and specific instructions for visitor entrances. I was going to prison for the first time.

Shiela seemed to be quite confident as she led me to the first window behind bars. An attendant asked for our identification, our reason for the visit, our "prisoner's" name, and then gave us paperwork to fill out. After returning the documents, which were stamped and stapled, we were handed a number and name tags and told to wait in the orange plastic chairs. Others were already there. We were scheduled for 10:10 a.m. with a twenty-minute visit. Rules!

"Okay," Shiela began. "Here's how we'll do this. I'll stay here, and when you come back I'll go back to the intake supervisor and ask for a "family visit," which is another twenty minutes. That way, we both get our time with Tim. Okay?"

"Sure," I mumbled. "Just fine."

I fingered the Bible with a letter in it from me and a pair of new brown socks. Timothy was not allowed to wear his shoes (nor belt), so his socks were wearing out. Small gift; small gestures. Why hadn't I brought more? My mind raced with guilt that I was bringing so little to someone who had sacrificed so much.

"FIRE-SON!" yelled the attendant. That was me, as Friesen was mispronounced.

I showed my identification, again, and the attendant took me into a long hallway with multiple small doors—like offices. They were visitor cells. A man was in each one, I presumed. The guard opened a cell door. I walked in, and the door slammed shut behind me. There sat Tim in street clothes. He smiled at me and said, "Bet you didn't expect to be in prison today!"

"Hardly," I managed. I was choked up. He was calm, as usual, and totally at peace. "How are you?"

"Great!" came the cheerful answer. "What's happening in your life?" And that began a quick twenty minutes as we talked about his kids, the church, and the conditions in prison (boredom, reading lots of books, non-vegetarian food, and interesting conversations). "This is not a place to get better if you've got problems. I'm here for a good reason, and no one is bothering me. It's a strict atmosphere, and I found lots of books in the library."

"Here's a Bible with a letter in it. No one asked to look at this, so I assume I can leave it with you."

I wondered, could I have brought a knife? Drugs? No guard had searched the Bible.

"Oh, they gave you a red visitor name tag. That means you are clergy. They don't hassle priests. Lucky you!"

In my mind, I still wondered how a female pastor got in the cell with a male prisoner with so little drama. I did see the security camera up in the ceiling corner, and I guessed the guard was standing just outside the closed door.

The twenty minutes passed, and I stood to leave Tim in the room sparsely furnished with two chairs and a table. He hugged me and thanked me. There were tears in his eyes.

"Bless you, Tim. You are loved by God and by your church. We will see you soon. Bye!" I exited the room and followed the guard back to the visitor waiting room. Shiela took her twenty-minute turn, and we traveled two hours back to our Kansas homes.

Spilling blood has consequences—some immediate, some eternal.

The Army and Me

"Madam Reverend, you are called to testify in the case of Henry Anderson. You have just affirmed your intention to tell the truth. Please be seated."

Yes, I would thankfully like to sit. My knees were shaking, and I was the only woman in a large room of men. My navy suit, crisp white blouse, and high heels were a sharp contrast to the sea of green with chest pins and brass buttons. Even though it was a mid-morning hearing time, I was already tired. I had driven into Fort Riley and maneuvered my car through checkpoints and security patrols.

"Ma'am, what brings you on the base?" was the police officer's question as he peered into my opened car window at the large stop sign indicating that I was now on federally protected land.

"I'm here to be a witness in a hearing at the request of Chaplain Murphy." I reached for the paperwork and handed him the official letter.

After a quick look at the letter, he said, "Thank you, ma'am. Please continue to the left and park in the zone marked 'Visitor' at Building D."

I did as he requested, but driving alone onto a huge army base for the first time tested my gut as well as my theology. What's a woman pastor doing here? I got out of my car and walked toward Building D. My heels clicked on the cement, and cat-calls and whistles sounded from the street as a group of green-uniformed men walked by. I quickened my step, entered the large assigned building, and looked for Hearing Room A. I sat down behind a large desk and faced three officers, all in uniform with stacks of folders by their desks.

"Tell us how long you have known Private Anderson."

"About six months."

"And tell us your relationship with Private Anderson."

"I am his pastor. He contacted me by telephone in late February inquiring about our congregation's worship time and our doctrine concerning pacifism. I explained the long Mennonite history concerning participation in war and our current practice of teaching conscientious objection to killing. Because of that phone call, Henry came to worship with our congregation in Manhattan. He and I had long conversations about his growing unease and finally his clear Christian decision to apply for a dismissal from the army based on his conscientious objector (CO) beliefs. And, by the way, he moved off base and has lived with our family for the past three months."

"Would you say he is sincere in his beliefs?"

"Most certainly. While he grew up in the Assembly of God Christian denomination and firmly believed in service to his country in the armed forces, he has studied the Bible and even sought out a pacifist Mennonite denomination to assist him in filing the correct forms seeking his separation from the army. This is a thoughtful, respectful young man. His young wife and baby have already gone to Illinois to live with her parents, as he does not wish for them to live in army housing. He misses his family but is committed in his desire to claim the CO status."

The next officer took over the questioning. "Reverend Friesen, thank you for coming here today. In your experience, does Private Anderson display religious beliefs that are Mennonite?"

I had to think quickly. Henry had told me many times over the past months that he did not approve of women pastors. He quoted scripture passages to me and demanded my biblical authority to preach. We, he said, were simply going to disagree, but he commended me on my pastoral care, my ability to work with the necessary separation paperwork, and my connections with the General Conference Mennonite Church Office of Peace and Justice—staffed by a former military officer and now a convinced Anabaptist and Mennonite seminary graduate. My mind was racing. "Was he a Mennonite?"

I, however, didn't want to share my personal irritation with Henry, which had grown while he lived with us, because that might taint my character witness. I was especially agitated when he decided to turn vegetarian after he saw me cooking using the "More-with-Less Cookbook." He didn't know a green bean from a pinto bean! I remembered telling Henry he could eat what he wanted, but I was not totally changing our family's eating habits nor was I going to cook for him. "Help yourself, buy your food. You may stay with us, but your new-found diet is your decision and I am not your housewife!" Yet his decision to become a pacifist was clearly profound and deep.

"Sir," I began carefully. "Henry entered the army a Christian. He began to doubt his ability to stay in the army during basic training when he was participating in exercises that included handling a gun for killing purposes. He asked to be a chaplain's assistant rather than a soldier on the field. He gradually came to a sincere belief in pacifism. He is not Mennonite. He opposes ordaining women as clergy, but he respects me for being ordained in the Mennonite denomination. So, sir, while he and I differ in some theological positions, I do not doubt his sincere pacifism, which actually happened here at Fort Riley."

The questioning passed to the third officer, who was obviously reading the completed application and pages of written testimony. "I have no questions. I thank you for your thoughtful responses and for your care of one of our soldiers. You are an honor to the military."

I nearly choked. I was an honor to the military? Really, not! I kept quiet. I needed to remain focused because Henry's application could mean an eventual release from the army or a court martial and jail time for the rest of his nearly three-year commitment.

I was dismissed, and I retraced my steps and route home. I sat in my office that day wondering what the officers would decide. They had thirty days to rule.

In the end, Henry was granted a CO classification and he left our home and congregation.

About a year later, I got a long letter from Henry. He was exploring other religions and considering seminary.

I never heard from him again.

My Pretty Little Head

My home phone rang just after 5:00 p.m. on a Friday afternoon.

"Oh no," I thought, "there's been a death."

It was not a death call but rather a puzzled staff member of the church who was paid a paltry sum for her bookkeeper hours.

"Dorothy, I was checking my mailbox and there was no paycheck today. It's the end of the month, and usually my check is there. Do you have it?"

"Sure don't. Did you check around the office? Maybe it's on the secretary's desk. I got my check, so I know the treasurer made them out."

She hung up, and I was puzzled but not troubled.

Then, about an hour later, the administrative assistant, a full-time female employee, called me at home.

"Dorothy, I didn't get my paycheck. It's not in my mailbox. Do you have it?"

With that, I knew I had a problem. Never were paychecks late nor misplaced in my short tenure at the congregation. Had someone stolen checks? Was there some kind of mix-up? I would call the treasurer.

My phone call to Max was short and included a startling confession.

"Of course, I wrote most of the paychecks. But we have a bit of a cash flow situation this month, so I decided which staff were to be paid. I wrote checks for all the men, but I decided that several women have husbands who have good jobs, so I'm waiting for another Sunday's offering before I write more checks. I'll get to them as soon as I feel better about our cash balance. Anyway, you shouldn't worry your pretty little head about finances."

I was so stunned I could hardly speak. Finally, I summoned a short response, "Figure out how to pay the staff immediately. We can't function this way, and this causes hurt feelings in the team."

I hung up, swallowing hard. There were so many layers of wrong in his decision, his attitude, and his patriarchal style. I was fuming. I stomped around my kitchen with fists clenched, screaming, "You have got to be kidding," and possibly some other words. As head of the staff, I was insulted and disregarded. He did not think he should even consult me before making an independent decision.

With that, I called the chair of the Staff Relations Committee and promptly told him the plight of the paychecks. "Fix this," was my command—and he assured me he would contact the treasurer and get things straightened out. By Sunday, all paychecks had been issued. The women thanked me. I never shared the treasurer's actions with any staff.

I also kept a close watch on the treasurer's attitude. The following Sunday, I included a casual quip in our conversation: "Sure glad we got that paycheck problem solved. Let's hope we never have to deal with that again."

He simply nodded.

Easter Comes Early for Imogene

Her name was Imogene. She was well known among the clergy of the city. Dressed in an assortment of polyester layers with gaudy costume jewelry, Imogene was a sight to behold. A tall woman with ridiculously high heels, she always came into the church building by herself, leaving her husband to sit in the car—which they dared not shut off for fear they wouldn't get it started again.

"Oh, pastor," she gushed, "It's just a miracle that you are here today. I have an emergency."

Of course, I knew her emergencies were always medical in nature— another hernia surgery, "terr'ble, poundin' headaches," or, heaven forbid, running out of insulin and "you know what that would mean."

"Come on in, Imogene. What seems to be the problem?"

The story, this time, was a lost check in the mail, an empty medicine bottle, and a husband who would certainly die without the precious capsules that "just keep his heart going." Could I spare thirty dollars from the church's emergency fund?

"And you know, Preacher Dorothy, when my inheritance comes through, your church will get back all the money you've loaned to me. I don't know what I would do if I couldn't get help from you. And I'll pay you back. You'll see."

I checked my notebook and saw that it had been awhile since Imogene had paid me a call, and the Mennonites were often on her six-month rotation. This time I decided to be firm.

"Imogene, here's the situation. I'll help you out this time. It's after 5:00 on Friday, and there's no way I can call the social security office to see about the delay with your check. (Why, oh why, do I stay in the office at that time, especially on Good Friday?) I'll phone them on Monday. Here's thirty dollars, but this is the last 'loan' I can give you for one year. Our church simply has other people it wants to help. I'm sure you understand."

157

Imogene put up no fuss but eagerly reached out her red-coated fingernails, as if to snatch this gold.

"So grateful to you, preacher. You people are so good. Well, gotta' go. Max is tired of sitting, and we have to get to filling the prescription. Sure hope my asthma don't hit again. I sorta' feel like I'm breathing funny." And with a weary gasp, she was gone.

My secretary and I watched as a tired, beat-up 1962 Ford chugged out of the parking lot, spewing smoke from the tailpipe and sounding like an ancient John Deere. We both speculated that the car might be on its deathbed and the next request might be for its health.

The rest of the weekend was a blur of activities with play practices, special music rehearsals, Easter sunrise service, potluck breakfast, and intergenerational activities celebrating the glorious resurrection.

It was Easter Monday when I picked up the newspaper to read, "Local woman wins lottery" in front page headlines. I glanced over the column quickly until "Imogene" caught my eye. I was flabbergasted. Imogene had won a $25,000 jackpot in the "Saturday Sweepstakes." She was quoted about her "terrible life but good luck" and "new home in Kentucky."

The righteous indignation in me could not be checked. Why did she waste her money on lottery tickets? And did I supply her with that winning dollar? I was fuming. The gall! The total and utter ridiculousness of it all. How could such an irresponsible person be so lucky? How could such an undeserving person receive such a huge gift?

I stood in my office for just a minute and then rushed to the secretary's office to show her the headline. There, a familiar noise of a sputtering car in the parking lot caught our attention. Imogene! She was back.

Right then, I decided that maybe she was settling the debt she had promised to repay. I softened.

Imogene rushed in, as usual, and was beaming. However, she only asked to use the phone. No demands. No thanks. No loan repayment. No nothing. Just a request to use the phone.

"Of course, Imogene. Here's my phone. I'll be in the front office."

"Just a minute, preacher," Imogene pleaded. "I really need help. Do you know a good lawyer? You see, I won this money, but I'm not about to let my good-for-nothing husband get one red cent of it. I'm going to divorce him. Then I'm off to Kentucky. Always wanted to live there. In fact, we're on our way. All packed up. Think I'll build me a dream home there. I feel so lucky!"

I didn't have the heart to explain to her about the legal rights of a spouse to good fortune, earned or not, but I halfheartedly showed her the yellow pages and simply let her find her way.

In a few minutes, she was ready to leave, irritated with the lawyers who wouldn't help her in her mischief. She hugged me and thanked me over and over for all the help I'd given to her.

Her farewell speech was a mixture of eloquence and gibberish. I can't remember it all anymore. Something about the Lord loving the poorest of the poor. Something about those good preachers who always helped her out. Something about Max and her kids and how Easter was pretty special. And maybe I'm just imagining it, but I think she said something about how wonderful it is to get something you really don't deserve. And with a "Praise the Lord," Imogene was gone.

Easter had come early for Imogene. I determined that if the church's dollar had brought her this moment, well, maybe the resurrection is more about that kind of undeserved grace than anything else.